FOOLS
CROW

FOOLS CROW

WISDOM
and POWER

THOMAS E. MAILS

COUNCIL OAK BOOKS, TULSA

———

Council Oak Books
Tulsa, Oklahoma 74120

© 1991 by Thomas E. Mails

Printed in the United States of America
97 96 95 94 93 92 91 90   5 4 3 2 1

Library of Congress Catalog Card Number 90-85350
ISBN 0-933031-35-1

Book design by Karen Slankard
Illustrations by Thomas E. Mails
Cover by Carol Haralson

———

To all the little hollow bones,
past, present, and future.
                    Thomas E. Mails

Anyone who is willing to live the life I have led
can do the things I do.
                    Fools Crow

Contents

1 THE OLD LORD OF THE HOLY MEN

WHAT YOU ARE ABOUT TO READ MAY BE THE RAREST DOCUment ever published about a Native American holy man. I do not mean to suggest by this claim that the quality of my writing deserves such merit — only that to my knowledge no other eminent holy person has ever, or perhaps could ever, so plainly have revealed how he knew what he knew and how he did the things that he did. Most of us would call his performance and life a miracle, although he would not. To him, miracles were the norm for life in the world, and, *Wakan-Tanka* having promised them, the true miracles would be if they had not happened

Frank Fools Crow told me one summer day in 1975 that he considered his uncle, the famous Black Elk, to be supreme among Sioux holy men. Many Sioux, however, see these two men standing together at the top of the holy-person pyramid, and in my view it is Fools Crow who may have been the greatest Native American holy person to live during the last one hundred years. Supporting this position are: the fact that while Black Elk was still alive and only sixty-five years of age, it was Fools Crow who, in 1925, was chosen to be the Ceremonial Chief of the Teton Sioux; the fact that Fools Crow alone was able to provide me with the disclosures in this book; and, while Black Elk was able to relate the details of the origin of the Sun Dance, there is no indication that he was ever an Intercessor for them as Fools Crow was.

While we were working together to compile the story of his life, Fools Crow gave me two kinds of related information. The first kind consisted of things that he felt his Creator God, *Wakan-Tanka*, wanted him to reveal before he died, and the second kind of things that were to be revealed posthumously —which factored in when he departed on November 27, 1989, at the age of 99 — more than twice the average life-span of Sioux living on the Pine Ridge and Rosebud reservations in South Dakota today.

Under the title *Fools Crow*, Doubleday & Company published the first body of material in 1979. It is a journal of his life, but includes descriptions of many of the extraordinary things *Wakan-Tanka* and the helper Powers did through him. In reissuing the book in 1990, the University of Nebraska Press describes its contents as follows: "Frank Fools Crow, a spiritual and civic leader of the Teton Sioux, spent nearly a century helping those of every race. A disciplined, gentle man who upheld the old ways, he was aggrieved by the social ills he saw besetting his own people and forthright in denouncing them. When he died in 1989 at the Pine Ridge Reservation in South Dakota, he was widely loved and respected. *Fools Crow* is based on interviews conducted in the 1970s. The holy man tells Thomas E. Mails about his eventful life, from early reservation days when the Sioux were learning to farm to later times when alcoholism, the cash economy, and World War II were fast eroding the old customs. He describes his vision quests and his becoming a medicine man. The Yuwipi and sweatlodge ceremonies, the Sun Dance, and instances of physical healing are related in memorable detail, and because Fools Crow lived joyfully in this world, so are his travels abroad and with Buffalo Bill's Wild West show, his happy marriages, his movie work, and his tribal leadership. He lived long enough to mediate between the U.S. government and Indian activists at Wounded Knee in 1973 and to plead before a congressional subcommittee for the return of the Black Hills to his people."

The information given in *Fools Crow* is exceedingly valuable, and it lays the necessary foundation for the rest of the material. To get the complete picture, those who read this book must also read it, since I do not duplicate its contents. I only repeat here what I am required to set the stage. But *Fools Crow* is not so dynamic or rare as this book, which alone reveals in amazing detail precisely *how* he did what he did, and *why* he was able to soar above other medicine people to become an exceptional tube for the Higher Powers to work in and through him. Its even greater dynamic is that it shows us how to become the same thing.

Some people will wonder why Fools Crow chose to entrust me with this extraordinary information. Both of us knew the question would be raised, and with the assistance of our friend and interpreter, Dallas Chief Eagle, we discussed it more than once, finding that we were in complete agreement about what The Creator wishes us to do with His gifts to humankind.

"The power and ways," Fools Crow said, "are given to us to be passed on to others. To think or do anything else is pure selfishness. We only keep them and get more by giving them away, and if we do not give them away we lose them." Black Elk's statements to John Neihardt and Joseph Epes Brown make it clear that he shared Fools Crow's view, and because of this freely imparted sacred knowledge to the two authors.[1] For those who are wondering, Fools Crow did share some of his knowledge and expertise with other medicine men, and there is some information about this in the *Fools Crow* book. But all of those mentioned are gone now, and have been for many years. Fools Crow outlived every one of them. During the times when he and I were together, he did not invite other medicine men to sit with us. It was apparent that, as much as he appeared in public and as

---

[1] Brown reports that Black Elk asked him to stay so that he might record an account of their religion. "The old man knew that he was soon to die, and he did not wish that this sacred lore, much of which he alone knew, should pass away with him." Brown, *The Sacred Pipe*, pp. X and XII.

accessible as he was to his people, Fools Crow was also a very private man where his preparation and practice of curing and healing were concerned.

Perhaps I can best explain the relationship that Fools Crow and I had by the fact that he asked me to call him by his first name, Frank, and not "grandfather," or "grandpa," as everyone else did. He knew that I had not come to sit at his feet to be his student or patient, and that he was never, in any sense, my mentor. At his request, our relationship was for him to tell me his story and for me to write it. While he intuitively knew when we first met that I was a writer, he also learned very quickly that I was a Lutheran pastor who believed firmly in Jesus Christ, and he accepted, as I do, that both of us knew and worshiped the same God — although by different names.

Fools Crow was baptized in the Roman Catholic Church at the age of twenty-five. Before I met him, he and his wife, Kate, had been attending mass fairly regularly at a Pine Ridge parish. But he remained a staunch traditionalist, and in his later years the frequency of attendance decreased. Whenever we were staying together in a town or city, Dallas Chief Eagle attended mass, but Fools Crow did not go with him. There was never a question as to which came first with Fools Crow, and I suspect that the parish priests knew this too. He did not believe that he could educate me about God or the Bible. He thought of me as an equal where these were concerned, and he did not attempt to teach me about things I already knew — he only explained what was necessary for me to articulate his story to others. He could not do this in English himself, and he knew that *Wakan-Tanka* wanted him to have someone who communed with the same God he did, so that he would not need to explain everything. Somehow, and the methods used are revealed herein, *Wakan-Tanka* told Fools Crow that I was that one who could and would do this, and I suspect that Black Elk was told the same thing where Neihardt and Brown were concerned. Considering that the two holy men put everything else in His hands, I doubt they would make such an important decision on their own. However it came about, I am delighted that it did. Fools Crow did not attempt to make a Native American traditionalist out of me, and I did not seek to influence him in Christian things. Sometimes he did ask me questions about the Bible and Christ, but simply to help his own understanding.

Among the Sioux and other Native Americans, Fools Crow is known as one of the few untouchables. What this means is that while many of those claiming to be authentic medicine persons have been and are suspect, he remained above reproach. He could not, even by those who were the most jealous of his position and accomplishments, be faulted in any way, and the nature of his funeral service attests most eloquently to this truth. What Fools Crow needed above all for this second kind of information was someone to help him draw out and shape what he had learned and experienced over a period of ninety-nine years — including his original vision quest as a boy, touching on his time with his main teacher, Stirrup, and covering his unbroken relationship with *Wakan-Tanka* and His Helpers. He listened intently to the instructions of the latter, and in typical Native American fashion, memorized them. Then he followed them to the letter. Ordinarily, it would not have occurred to him to ask why things were done, or to organize, formulate and think through what he learned so that he could answer the questions of others —especially those of non-Indians — although for the sake of posterity he wanted to answer mine as well as he could. No doubt he had known for decades that when it came time to do the story of his life and work he would have to make this concession. Constant contact with non-Indians would have taught him that we outsiders are a "how? and why?" group . . . that we search constantly for understanding and want to be shown. Even though he regretted this non-Indian trait, for *Wakan-Tanka's* and our sakes, he accommodated himself to it. Much of this will be a surprising revelation for those who have believed that the Native American medicine people are not able to analyze their understandings, or to articulate these to outsiders. As will be seen, however, Fools Crow did an uncommonly good job of it, and his wisdom is powerful.

For this second kind of information, his procedure was, with the able assistance for the most part of Dallas, to give, as well as he could, answers to questions that I formulated. Then he had Dallas and me help him shape this into expressions he was satisfied with. He talked, we listened, we probed for fuller development, I wrote, I read it back

to him, and only when he was satisfied that I had said what he wished me to say, did we go on. Most of my evenings were spent pulling together each day's work. It was drudgery, but in the end it achieved what we both wanted. So then, this book — even when quotation marks are used — is seldom precisely what Fools Crow said, but rather what I helped him say. Even as I write now, I am forced to edit and choose words. That fact may disturb some readers, since it suggests that I might have shaped what is written to fit my own ideas. But I have little to gain by that, and have been careful not to do it. Dallas' presence provided added assurance in that wise. Such situations simply cannot be avoided unless all parties speak both languages fluently, and even then perceptions are involved.

I am certain that this was also the case when, using an interpreter, John Neihardt expressed in English what Black Elk told him in the Lakota language. No matter how hard a writer tries and how sincere he is, the people he depicts come off somewhat different than they really are. In testimony to this truth, I once, without telling him who the book was about, read to Fools Crow parts of *Black Elk Speaks*. After awhile, he asked me quizzically, "Who is this man you are reading about?" When I told him he shook his head in a negative way and said, "That is not my uncle." He did not mean by this that Niehardt's account was fraudulent, or that the material was biased. He meant only that it did not sound like the voice he was so familiar with. It is for this reason that my *Fools Crow* book is quite plain as compared to the literary quality of the classic *Black Elk Speaks*, penned by the eloquent poet laureate of Nebraska. I wanted mine to sound as much like the real-life Fools Crow as was possible. My treatment of the songs Fools Crow gave me is consistent with the above. The terse nature of songs in the original language can be baffling for those who are not familiar with Lakota word associations. So my song translations are not literal. Nevertheless, their final wording was satisfactory to Fools Crow, and what I have written has his blessing.

There is no purpose to be served by relating in each instance where exactly Fools Crow and I were when this second kind of information was given. It happened at his home, at Bear Butte, in motels, when we were on our way somewhere or coming back, during ceremonies, or while we were out praying together. It was usually an extension of that which was cited in the first book. The manner in which it came to me was always the same. Fools Crow did not specifically say that certain material was to be withheld until after his death. Instead, while we were talking about some subject he would hold up both hands palms forward to stop the conversation for a moment and as an indication that I should turn off the tape recorder. From then until he finished I was to use only my notebooks. If he was doing a ritual to show me how something was done, I had to remember it and reconstruct it as best I could after the ritual was over. Truly, I did not know whether this second kind of material would ever be published. I might have gone before he did although I think he knew I would outlive him, else he would not have entrusted me with it. As it is, though, nearly 15 years have gone by since it was first received.

This book consists of things not too sacred to tell, but too personal to tell. It was his opinion that special gifts are given to each individual for use during their lifetime. Yet they can, at any time they feel they should or that *Wakan-Tanka* wants them to, retire from medicine work and pass on any or all of these gifts to a person or people they consider worthy to receive them, including the songs that go with them — "worthy" being measured by the manner of life the recipients lead and their devotion to *Wakan-Tanka* and the work — with the added condition always being that it must be done for the sake of others.

Careful observers will find many similarities between the things Fools Crow told me and the practices of other Native American tribes. In most instances, he did not know from personal observation that the similarities existed, because his contacts with medicine people outside the Great Plains area were quite limited. He was given some information about other tribes by visitors such as myself, and he was a good learner.

When I asked him why similarities exist between tribes, his answer was a firm, "All of us are taught by the same God, so we should expect to find the same teachings and practices everywhere.[2] The only differences would be determined by where people have lived and what means were available to them. Long before writing came to us, we learned by observing the seasons and nature, by experiencing and studying with the elders, and by listening to the Higher Ones. In the beginning they taught our ancestors things which were to be passed down from generation to generation. Only rarely do we hear the actual voices of *Wakan-Tanka* and His Helpers, although I do when I spirit travel, and I have heard His voice twice in visions. Mostly, I receive their directions and advice through meditating with concentration tools, and through signs or things other people say to me. Once I pray and use my self-offering stick, I know that the answer is on its way

---

[2] At a symposium in Canada in 1977, Allan Wolf Leg, a Blackfoot and a Roman Catholic, said, "The heritage, the philosophies, the message that came from God through Nature to the Indian people, these are the same as what Jesus Christ means to Christians. God came through Jesus Christ and his disciples to the people just as He came through His agents in Nature to the Indian people. The latter is called paganism . . . Yet there is no difference. It is the same God." *Native Religious Traditions, Symposium of Elders and Scholars*, Edmonton, Alta., 1977.

to me, and I am constantly looking for it as I go about my daily tasks or perform a ritual."

Something else everyone should know about Fools Crow is that he was taught, and accepted, that *Wakan-Tanka* has a form and is not a blob or an indefinable something whose being is spread uniformly throughout the universe. Fools Crow believed that in order for us to love the Creator He has to have a form we can imagine, or at least feel, although finite beings cannot know until after they have died what an infinite Being looks like. And so, no graven images of *Wakan-Tanka* or the Helpers are to be made. Statements that relate to this view are scattered throughout the following material — some of which might give readers fits as they attempt to reconcile them. For example, Fools Crow has already hinted that he spirit-traveled to the places where the Higher Powers dwell, and so would have seen them. As he describes these experiences more fully farther on you must remember that the reconciliation of data is seldom a concern of medicine people. It comes from God and that is enough. They simply accept what happens, bathe in the wonder of it, and then act upon it. A book like this is an exception in that it forced Fools Crow to reconcile his information, and we discover that he did so amazingly well. But ordinarily the medicine people do not waste time with the whys and wherefores, leaving this entirely up to those who find reward in such things. Meanwhile, the endless search and research progresses out here and aching individuals remain unhealed and unfulfilled, while Fools Crow and his kind were happy as could be.

Fools Crow was also a willing dependent where *Wakan-Tanka* and his Helpers were concerned. He saw nothing diminishing about this. He knew that *Wakan-Tanka*, "The Highest and Most Holy One," gives people magnificent minds and natural power that they are expected to use — but he also recognized that putting ourselves completely in God's infinitely capable hands is for our own best good. Our accepting this fact is essential to our understanding and participating in the timeless Native American pathways. Spirituality has infused and influenced every aspect of traditional Native American life. For them, there has been no such thing as purely secular life. Hunting is a spiritual adventure. Even art work and crafts are prayed into being, and it has been a life-way that leads to profound respect and reverence for nature. The ancient Native American people lived cooperatively, didn't waste, didn't litter or pollute on the scale we do, and most were involved in far less warfare than is generally believed. There was no need for them to have an "Earth Day" as we are having now to alert people to the perils that have come into being. Every day was a day of earth preservation for them. Saying this is not a naive ennoblement of the ancient Native Americans, it is a statement of fact. Even though there were as many as 10 million of them in North America at the time of European intrusion, there is not one shred of evidence that they despoiled the environment in any way of consequence. Everywhere the Europeans went, they found a pristine wilderness of crystal clear waters and burgeoning forests. After thousands of years of human habitation there were still nowhere near the number of endangered species of animals, fish or birds that there are today. Some anthropologists believe that Paleo Indians, who developed stone spearpoints, wiped out mastodons, sloths, saber-toothed cats, and some other species. But whatever role the Indians played, it is nothing compared to what non-Indians have wrought since the late Pliestocene age.

Despite the legion of exceptional things that were accomplished through Fools Crow, the eulogies since his death have highlighted his profound love and concern for all races. People recognize both his fervent wish to share God's gifts with as many as he could reach, and the fact that he pitied others who did not understand why this must be so. "The survival of the world," he said, "depends upon our sharing what we have and working together. If we don't, the whole world will die. First the planet, and next the people." Then he added, "The ones who complain and talk the most about giving away medicine secrets are always those who know the least." He had little time for anyone who attempted to keep blessings to themselves.

Fools Crow and Black Elk were convinced that the Supreme Being they worshiped was the One True God of the Bible — which was an even stronger reason to share gifts with all people.[3] Sadly

[3] "I shall explain," Black Elk said, "what our pipe really is; peace may come to those peoples who can understand, an understanding which must be of the heart and not of the head alone. Then they will realize that we Indians know the One True God, and that we pray to Him continually." Brown, 1953, p. XX.

though, it has taken centuries for any of the Christian churches to recognize both this truth of a common God and the fact that Christians can learn a great deal about spirituality from the Native Americans. For more than twenty years I have been stating this publicly with only limited response, therefore I am delighted to report that at long last some of the leaders of mainline churches are recognizing it. Consider, for example, the following portion of a stunning report:

On October 16, 1988, and where the Christian church is concerned more than three centuries too late, the *Seattle Times* carried a long article describing how the area bishops and other leaders of ten major mainline church groups (two Lutheran, two Catholic, Methodist, Presbyterian, Baptist, United Church of Christ, Christian Church, and Episcopal) had offered a formal written apology to native people for the churches' long-standing participation in the destruction of traditional Native American spiritual practices, and made a pledge to help Native American and Eskimo peoples reclaim and protect the legacy of their traditional religious teachings, asking for forgiveness and blessings. "The spiritual power of the land and the ancient wisdom of your indigenous religions can be, we believe, great gifts to the Christian churches. We offer our commitment to support you in the righting of previous wrongs; to protect your peoples' efforts to enhance native spiritual teachings; to encourage the members of our churches to stand in solidarity with you on these important religious issues . . . We call upon our people for recognition of and respect for your traditional ways of life and for protection of your sacred places and ceremonial objects. We have frequently been unconscious and insensitive and not come to your aid when you have been victimized by unjust federal policies and practices. In many other circumstances we reflected the rampant racism and prejudice of the dominant culture with which we too willingly identified . . . May the God of Abraham and Sarah, and the Spirit who lives in both the Cedar and Salmon people, be honored and celebrated . . ."

What these church leaders do not admit is that it has been mainly through church actions that most of the Native American religious traditions have been eradicated, are irretrievably lost, and that the consequent cost to Native Americans and the world is enormous.

When I attended Luther Theological Seminary (now Luther-Northwestern Theological Seminary) in the 1950s no one on the teaching staff ever once mentioned Native Americans. Today, the situation has changed considerably. Last year, the *Minneapolis Star and Tribune* featured a full-page article by staff writer, Martha Sawyer Allen, that was captioned, "Indian, Christian Faiths Fuse." Since the newspaper used my book, *Sundancing at Pine Ridge and Rosebud*, for its pictorial details, and without asking my permission (although they did credit the material), I will cite portions of their very informative text.

The article mentions The Rev. Steve Charleston, a Choctaw who teaches cross-cultural studies at Luther Northwestern Seminary, and who argues that Indians have a sacramental tradition that is as valid as — and in many ways similar to — that of the Old Testament Hebrew tribes, the fountainhead of Christianity. Charleston is considered by many to be the main architect for a new theology, and says, "He (Jesus) arises from Native America, claims the gospel for us, and now our job as Native American Christians is to evangelize the western world with a revolutionary and reformed vision of what the church will be in the next century . . . God came to earth once, in the form of Jesus, but came to all people." The new theology is described as a "hybrid religion" that "has roots in both Christian and traditional Indian beliefs and is evolving into a theology that binds people in sacramental kinship. Its adherents are whites and Indians who are finding ways to combine holy and sacred elements from both traditions."

This new theology, the article continues, is being created by the second generation of Indian seminary graduates. These are deeply versed in traditional rituals and can talk with authority to white clerics. One of these (graduates), the Rev. Marlene Helgemo, a Winnebago, is associate pastor at University Lutheran Church of Hope in Minneapolis. She is quoted as saying, ". . . We [Christians and Traditionalists] all believe there is only one God, and we need to raise up the questions that new theologians need to be answering." Helgemo participates in a Sun Dance every year at the Rosebud Reservation, and is hoping that the new theology will follow the Sun Dance outline (I give in some of my other books and herein the essence of the Sun

Dance as only Fools Crow truly knew it, including the grand secret of a way he had to renew and regenerate himself in Sun Dance fashion at a moment's notice). "We need," she continues, "more coming of the human community in a circle, sharing concerns and prayer. The world needs more sun dances."

Featured also in the *Star and Tribune* article is the Rev. Virgil Foote, a Lakota and an Episcopal priest, whose Mazakute Memorial Church is in St. Paul. He practices both Christianity and his Lakota religion passionately, arguing that following his native ceremonies has made him a better Christian. "When I pray," he says, "I pray in Lakota and English. Our people need to hear there is truth in both. I'm a Lakota, I'm a Christian. I'm one in the same. I pray to one God."

Perhaps as you read this you can hear me sighing to myself — how many times over the past twenty-five years have I said this identical thing? . . . and that being able to look at spiritual truths through the eyes of medicine acquaintances has opened some Bible verses for me in ways that my seminary professors never did while I was there.

Foote has danced and even pierced in the Sun Dance at Rosebud — at that place where, at Fools Crow's and Eagle Feather's urging, I recorded its every detail for posterity. A few people complained about what I was doing then. I wonder whether they are complaining now. Those two foremost Intercessors (dance leaders) knew what they were doing in asking me, and clearly understood that the recording was *Wakan-Tanka's* will. That is true also of the *Fools Crow* book, and of *Fools Crow: Wisdom and Power*.

"I wish," Foote says, "that I had done all this before I went to the seminary. I would have known the Bible better, understood the life of Christ in a much deeper way . . . At the Sun Dance . . . you get in touch with your physical and spiritual self and respect the sacred in everything." Well, Fools Crow was there waiting, and he tried to tell his people. . . .

The article closes with two more insights that deserve repeating, especially because Fools Crow made the same comments to me, and I have been stressing them in my Native American workshops. Both should be borne in mind as we consider what Fools Crow reveals in this book.

"Many whites in the ecology movement," the article says, "are attracted to Indian theology. Hundreds of others participate in sweatlodges in Minnesota and elsewhere . . . But these theologians worry that whites may be attracted to bits and pieces of the theology without understanding the whole . . . The Rev. Jim Egan, a white Jesuit, cautions that Christians must respect Indian theology and not just siphon off the 'interesting' rituals for their own use without following disciplines required for participation. Egan was keeper of the sweatlodge fire at the sun dance. A former Rosebud missionary, he now works at the Cenacle Retreat House in Wayzata. The second insight is that the new theologians encounter enormous problems, legacies of four hundred years of attempts to eradicate Indian culture. They are caught between the two worlds, traditional Indians and Indians who profess only Christianity. . . . The Indian rights movement of the 1970s spawned a concerted effort to preserve, honor, and practice Indian rituals and ways of life. More than half of all Indians now eschew Christianity, claim only their traditional ways, and bar whites from their ceremonies . . . The new theology has a long way to go before it is accepted by whites or Indians."

A few of the Indian people mentioned in the *Star and Tribune* article were at Sun Dances I attended, and learned some things at these and other dances that were being led by Fools Crow or Eagle Feather. But all of those mentioned would have profited greatly by being Fools Crow's full-time students. He knew and practiced for nearly a century what the just-mentioned clerics have only recently begun to conclude. I also believe that Black Elk and Fools Crow actually originated the "new theology," since they were the first to clearly point out what the clerics are saying, and more.

Having pursued this matter of Christian-traditional relationships as far as I have, it might be concluded that the rest of the book is permeated with references to it. That is not the case. All I have wanted to do is to fix in literary cement what amounts to one of the most incredible milestones in Christian church history — a stunning reversal of opinion where Native American religion is concerned. I harbor no illusions that such developments as these will escalate into anything like acceptance by all, or even a majority of, the Christian churches. But it is a strong beginning, and I, together with the Native Americans, am exceedingly grateful for it! Now though, everything that needs to be said about this has been said, and from here on the book is entirely Fools Crow.

Among the matters he and I discussed was that of people having closed minds which keep them from seeing marvelous things. In conjunction with this I told him a story I'd heard about a hunter who had been given a dog that could walk on water. When he wanted a witness who would support this fantastic claim, the only person available was an elderly farmer who seemed oblivious to what the dog was doing. After the dog had performed his amazing feat several times and the farmer said nothing, the frustrated hunter asked him if he hadn't noticed anything special about the dog. "Well," he drawled, "now that you mention it, that mutt can't swim!" Often, after this, when Fools Crow talked about how hard it was to get through to people, he would say something about "dogs walking on water," and slowly shake his head. I am about to complete the description of a holy man who did more than walk on water, and I hope that standard preconceptions will not keep anyone from seeing the greatness of his spectacular performance. The holy person I present here was not perfect, but he came as close to it as anyone I have ever known.

Once the *Fools Crow* book was finished, I saw less and less of him over the passing years. I returned to the Pueblo book I had interrupted to do his, and after that went on to research other books in places like Oklahoma, New Mexico, and Arizona. We did keep in touch, and I went to visit him at intervals to see how he was and to help where I could. Sometimes I took people to him who were anxious to meet him, or who hoped he would cure or heal them. Until his untimely death from a heart attack, Dallas Chief Eagle kept me apprised, and other friends at Rosebud did the same. Dik Darnell, a mutual friend of Fools Crow and myself, was with the old holy man often and probably did more to watch over and provide for him in his declining years than any other person. My good friend, the superb Oglala singer Buddy Red Bow, loved Fools Crow and always went out of his way to keep me informed about him. I remain indebted and grateful to all of these friends — especially for those times when they let me know that the holy man needed special help and I was able to assist them with it. Among those who came along after I did was John Denver, who from the time he first met Fools Crow became devoted to him and contributed even more than was needed.

The Fools Crow interviews were completed in 1977, and Fools Crow was already eighty-seven years of age. He was still amazingly strong and healthy, and was treating patients, leading Sun Dances, assisting and guiding his people, and always available for tribal events and needs. Kate, his second wife whom he married in 1958, was his stalwart supporter and assistant, although in later life she suffered several debilitating illnesses that concerned him greatly, especially because she never asked him in the traditional way with tobacco to heal her. Why she did not, he did not know, because she had seen him heal hundreds of people with conditions as bad or worse than hers, and in fact was with us when he did most of the things I saw him do. But he loved her dearly, and told me that when he lost her, as he knew he would before long, much of his reason for continuing on would be gone.

Fools Crow himself developed an arthritic condition in his knees that affected his mobility somewhat. It was hard for him to get to his feet from a sitting position, and also to sit down. He dropped down instead. Once he was up though, he moved about as well as ever.

I said to him one day, "Frank, you could heal those knees of yours if you wanted to."

"Yes," he answered, "but *Wakan-Tanka* has already been so good to me I don't have the heart to ask him for more."

A Canadian friend, who for personal reasons wishes to remain anonymous, wrote me a long letter about two visits he made to Fools Crow — one with his ailing mother in 1985, and another with his wife in 1987. Most of his beautiful letter is to remain confidential, and I will respect that wish. But there are things in it that will be helpful here. Also, included with the letter were two 1987 photographs of Fools Crow that show him to be well groomed, but much thinner than he was the last time I saw him.

This Canadian, whom I shall refer to as "Y," learned from a relative who was with Fools Crow at the time the photographs were taken that the holy man was no longer performing ceremonies, and that his medicine bundle had been passed on to a younger man. However, the recipient had since "lost the right to be a medicine man, and was dead." It seemed he had not taken the transfer of power seriously, and had suffered the consequences. To my consternation, no mention was made as to what had happened to the medicine bundle, and as I reveal in this book some of the wondrous things that were in it and the way they were used, I expect that my consternation will be broadly shared.

Y had brought Fools Crow several copies of the *Fools Crow* book, which he had been "lucky enough" to find in Toronto a few months before. "Fools Crow," Y states, "kissed the book and seemed very pleased to see it. [The numerous copies I gave Fools Crow always disappeared very quickly.] He motioned for me to sit beside him and turned to the drawing you had made of his vision experience inside the rock cliff at Bear Butte. Then he told me in English how he spoke to the animals, and he seemed very excited about it all over again. Fools Crow was glad to hear that the books were his and [said] there were friends he wanted to give one to. On the second visit I learned that one of them had been given to Matthew King, who you make several references to in the *Fools Crow* book."

Although Fools Crow was no longer doing ceremonies for curing during the time of Y's visits, the holy man went into his bedroom, which he unfortunately had to keep locked even when he was at home, and returned with pieces of unidentified root. The first time, in 1985, "He lit the end of the root with a match and waved it near my mother's face, telling her to breathe it in and that it would help her. It was clear to me," Y says, "that Fools Crow could perform a ceremony without being wrapped up. He had now reached a spiritual plane where this was possible."

During the second visit, Y himself was terminally ill, and Fools Crow gave him a dried plant together with instructions about how he should use it. "Fools Crow did not explain what the plant might be for, but repeated that it should be used exactly as directed." Three years later, at the time Y wrote to me, the plant was accomplishing its purpose and Y was still alive.

As indicated, I was stunned by the report that Fools Crow had passed on his medicine bundle, and knowing his perceptiveness, I am even inclined to doubt that he did, for he would have been able to see into the true heart of any man he might consider for that honor. Perhaps something else had happened to it that someone does not wish known. I know absolutely that, as of my last visit with him, he had not found anyone he felt he could entrust with the entire responsibility of being the Sun Dance Intercessor.[4] This does not, of course, mean that he did not find someone after that visit. But if anyone makes this claim, I would appreciate the opportunity to question him about some aspects of the dance that would tell me for certain whether he had the gift and the knowledge.

Nothing, however, would please me more than to learn there is indeed a legitimate heir, for the Sun Dance, as the new-theology people have realized, must continue and be done in the correct way. As it is, the deaths of Fools Crow and of his pupil, Eagle Feather, have at best left only a few among the Sioux who are properly equipped — a fact that has proven their wisdom in having me record the details of the Sun Dance in their entirety, rather than to have them lost. We can apply this lesson to all of the Native American traditional rituals, for with every passing day their continuance becomes more difficult and tenuous. Resurgences in tribal interest in ancient rites being what they may, except for the Zuni and the Eastern Pueblos, it will not be long before the only thing of consequence that is left will be what is recorded in books. Even among the Hopi, one of the last and greatest bastions of traditional life, the old structures are crumbling, and it might be worthwhile for us to take a moment to see in their religious demise how it has gone for the Sioux and so many other Native American tribes.

Only twenty years ago, after thousands of years of surviving on sparse crops and splendid rain dances that preserved a quiet and

---

[4] In *Fools Crow*, p. 137, I list the names of the men Fools Crow was training to do portions of the Sun Dance. On p. 169, Fools Crow expresses optimism that someone will take his place, but over the months we were together he vacillated between optimism and pessimism, never seeming to be certain as to how it would finally turn out.

peaceful society, the Hopi stepped fully into the modern age by selling, together with their Navajo neighbors, the Black Mesa rights for coal and water to a strip-mining company that provides the fuel for power plants that light up Southern California, Phoenix, Arizona, and Nevada. Already, while the Tribal government has grown dependent upon the Peabody Coal Mine's payments, Hopi water supplies are fast disappearing. Springs have dried up, wells have played out, and the one river that runs through the reservation has slowed down and turned salty. The ground water level of Kayenta, a community near the mine, has dropped forty-two feet since the mine opened.

Meanwhile, the Hopi Tribe has long been divided into those who oppose the mine, and those who want the money from it. For the few Hopi who work in the mine, there are trailer homes, telephones, televisions, trucks, and fast foods. They have less time than they formerly did to share in religious ceremonies. The changes have brought crimes, drinking, and drugs that were unheard of in prior years. Elders such as Thomas Banyacya, 83, trace nearly all of the problems to the mine. He believes that it has seriously weakened the religious life of the Tribe and threatens with extinction the ancient culture that has enabled them to survive.

Those who favor the mine believe that the amenities of life are more important than culture — especially when that culture has been marked by relative poverty. Yet even they must recognize that unemployment still exceeds forty percent, and average family income is only $5,000 a year.

What needs also to be considered is that as the mine plays out and their culture continues to erode, the Hopi will inevitably arrive at the day when, like the Sioux and other tribes, they will face the stark realization that their roots, center, and self-esteem have gone with it. When that happens, the money won't matter so much any more, and their Fools Crows will also be few and far between. Incidentally, it might be thought that the Western Sioux did not have a mine to sell. They did. It is called "The Black Hills of South Dakota," and they are more valuable today than the Black Mesa mine will ever be. The Hills had become the holy land of the Sioux, and ever since the Sioux traded it to the United States Government in 1868 for a pittance of reservation land, things have gone steadily downhill for them.

At least seven hundred mourners came to Fools Crow's funeral — an unusually large number for a burial at Pine Ridge, and a resounding testimony to the fact that he was greatly respected and loved. I am certain that everyone there had been comforted and served by him in one way or another, and that the seven hundred were only a fraction of the total number who were helped. But the attendance is also a testimony to something else we must not miss; something that will be dawning painfully upon everyone as time passes. The Sioux and other Native Americans have been pointing out in recent years that prior to white intrusion, holistic health and healing was a hallmark of Native American life. Also emphasized have been the outstanding virtues of traditional life and wisdom. The problem is, that while the oral evidence for this is available, the living evidences are, with the passage of time, fast disappearing. For the Sioux, Fools Crow may have been one of the last living proofs of what they profess. For the last one hundred years he has encompassed within himself and his manner of life everything that has been great about the people.

2 LITTLE HOLLOW BONES

THE GREAT HOLY MAN, BLACK ELK, SAID, "I CURED WITH THE power that came through me. Of course it was not I who cured. It was the power from the outer world, and the visions and ceremonies had only made me like a hole through which the power could come to the two-leggeds. If I thought that I was doing it myself, the hole would close up and no power could come through. Then everything I could do would be foolish."

As Fools Crow and I discussed the matter of how a person serves the Higher Powers, I asked, "Do you agree with Black Elk that the medicine person is a hole that *Wakan-Tanka* and the Helpers work through to help people?"

"We [Black Elk and he] talked about this several times. We agreed that the Higher Powers had taught us this same thing. We are just holes. But as I have used hollow bones for curing, I have decided that it is better to think of medicine people as little hollow bones."

"All medicine persons are hollow bones that *Wakan-Tanka*, *Tunkashila*, and the Helpers work through?"

"In and through. The power comes to us first to make us what we should be, and then flows through us and out to others."

I told him that Pueblo medicine men thought of themselves as tubes, and that I had been told by them how this worked out in their lives. I said it had captured my interest fully to hear him using this same terminology, and wondered whether, in his becoming a hollow bone, he went through the same four stages as they did — first calling in *Wakan-Tanka* to rid themselves of everything about them that will impede Him in any way — such as doubt, questions or reluctance; then recognizing themselves as a clean tube ready to be filled with hope and possibilities and anxious to be filled with power; then in the third stage experiencing the power as it comes surging into them; and finally giving the power away to others in the knowledge that, as they are emptied out, the Higher Powers will keep filling them with even greater power to be given away.[5] Although I did not say so, I wondered as I told him this whether it was possible that here on the Great Plains I would find the same concept. If Fools Crow knew and practiced this, it would be another proof of both our convictions that, since we know and worship the same God, it is natural to assume that He teaches all those who love Him the same basic lessons.

Fools Crow answered most of my questions the very next morning, when he asked me to go out with him to pray. On his left arm he carried a folded blanket, in his left hand a drum and drum stick, and in his right hand his pipe, his smoke (smudging) materials — this time a filled sea shell — and a golden eagle feather.

I should explain that Fools Crow did his smudging ("making smoke" he called it) in two ways. For personal situations, such as when he was smudging ritual items, he simply lit the end of a braided or twisted piece of sweetgrass and waved the sweetgrass around and over the items. If sweetgrass was not available, he used dried sage. For other circumstances where a greater quantity of smoke was

---

[5] For comparison, the Cahuilla tribe of California has believed that when medicine people come into their power they have to get rid of themselves, "as if peeling off old habits the way you peel an orange." They have to quit looking back and must go forward and be strong, "for the stream of life gets rough sometimes." Modesto and Mount 1980, p. 40.

needed, he made a mixture of sweetgrass, dried sage and tobacco in a large sea shell, and lit this. When the amount of smoke was sufficient, he blew occasionally on the hot ashes as he used the eagle feather to push the smoke toward others who were involved in the ceremony, and also toward the ritual items he would be using. As he pushed the smoke, he fluttered the feather, and did it so beautifully that when you closed your eyes you had the distinct sensation that an eagle was hovering close around you. If this was being done in the sweatlodge, you would even hear the shrill cry of the eagle.

When we reached the place where he customarily prayed, he refolded the blanket until it was rectangular in shape and perhaps a quarter of its unfolded size. Then he spread it out on the grass. He placed the filled sea shell at the east end of the blanket and on the northeast corner, then used a match to light it. When it was smoking well and the sweet smell of it was permeating the area, he used the feather to smudge first me, then himself, and finally the blanket. This done, he faced the east, removed his glasses, and knelt down on the blanket. It was seven a.m., and Sun was already up and bathing both the area and Fools Crow. His face glowed, and the sunlight smoothed away his wrinkles. He seemed to grow young again. He closed his eyes, and breathed deeply seven times to begin his immersion into the ritual he was about to perform. When he was done, he rested his cupped hands in his lap and listened for *Wakan-Tanka's* response.

While he did this, I pondered the idea of immersion, and what happens to the mind when you do it. The old holy man and other medicine people had taught me that the more time you spend and the deeper you go the greater the success of your quest. The entire idea has to do with achieving a state of complete communion with *Wakan-Tanka* and the Helpers. Once this is accomplished, They can enlighten and lead you, giving you comfort, strength, hope, and power. The amount of time spent in immersion is never wasted, and it reverses the usual procedure we follow when we are faced with time-consuming and critical chores. Ordinarily, we think we must rush and organize to get at the work because there is so little time. If we pray at all regarding the situation, it is only briefly, because we have so much to do. Then we spend the entire day working on the chores, and end up frustrated and drained. With immersion, you spend a lot of time in prayer, obtain from the Higher Powers the strength and guidance you need, and then finish those same chores in a fraction of the time, ending up fulfilled and fresh.

With his eyes still closed, Fools Crow began to pull with both hands at his chest and abdomen — as if he were pulling out evil or negative things. He grabbed many handfuls, and he threw away what he had seized.

Next, he stretched both arms and hands as high as he could up toward the sky and held them there for at least two minutes while he looked up and smiled broadly. He was as happy as ever I saw him.

After this, he began to clutch at the air above him, where he seized unseen things and shoved handfuls of them into his head and body.

Finally, he started to pull invisible things out of his chest and body, but this time he held both hands side by side in front of him and threw what he was clutching out to an invisible audience . . . invisible to me, that is, but visible to him I am sure.

No words were spoken while Fools Crow made these gestures, but when he was finished, he picked up the drum and beat it softly as he sang a "sound" song — that is, a song in which syllables were used to carry the melody, but which had no meanings. The beat was what the Lakota call the "parade beat," which is slow and steady, and is used for serious occasions. If Kate had been there, she would have "trilled" to express her happiness and appreciation.

When the song was finished, Fools Crow, still on his knees, pointed the stem of his pipe out to the Four Directions, up to *Wakan-Tanka* and *Tunkashila*, and down to Grandmother Earth. Then he turned to me and said, "*Wakan-Tanka* and the Helpers just made me a clean new hollow bone. Whenever there is time before I must begin to cure or heal a person, or before I am to lead or share in a ceremony, I go off by myself and ask Them to prepare me like this."

"You say *Wakan-Tanka* and *Tunkashila*," I said. "Most authorities consider these to be different names for the same Person."

"No!" Fools Crow replied adamantly. "We have three Chief Gods like the Christians do. *Wakan-Tanka* is like the Father. *Tunkashila* is like the Son. The Powers and Grandmother Earth together are like the Holy Spirit, and I call the five of them '*Wakan-*

Tanka's Helpers.' When I speak of all seven of the Beings together, I sometimes call them the 'Higher Powers.' When I pray with my pipe I point the stem up to *Wakan-Tanka*, then just a little lower to *Tunkashila*. But *Wakan-Tanka* and *Tunkashila* think, act, and watch over us as One. So there is only One God. Whenever I say, *Wakan-Tanka*, I mean *Tunkashila* too."[6]

"It appeared that you did four kinds of gestures," I said with unfeigned enthusiasm.

"Ho," he said as he held his clenched fists out in front of him. "First I thought about all of the stumbling blocks about me that can get in *Wakan-Tanka's* and the Helper's way when I want them to work in and through me. Then I asked them to remove these things so that I am a clean bone. They did this, and as I felt the obstacles coming out I grabbed them and threw them away. When all of this was done I felt fresh and clean. I saw myself as a hollow bone that is all shiny on the inside and empty. I looked around inside myself to see if any obstacles or junk were left, and there were none. I knew then that I was ready to serve *Wakan-Tanka* well, and I held up my hands to offer my thanksgiving and to tell Him how happy I was. Immediately, I could feel the power begin to come into me, and I reached up to help it. It was wonderful, and my energy grew until I was completely filled with power. Before long I thought I would explode! Then I saw people of all races all around me, and I gave the power away to them. All of them were very grateful, and it made me feel good to share in this giving. As I emptied myself out, I could feel more power coming into me, and it was wonderful!" He watched me carefully to see what my response would be. "That is how I become a little hollow tube," he said.

---

[6] See also *Fools Crow*, p. 58. This concept of a triune God is more common to the Indians than is ordinarily believed. When I was with a Zuni Clan Chief one evening, we talked about their War God. He drew me a picture of it, and explained that the largest figure was the same as the Father in Christian theology, the smaller figure tied to the larger one was the same as the Son, and the four large sticks tied to the larger figure were the same as the Holy Spirit. He went on to say that the War God not only aids the Zuni against human enemies, it also aids them against all forms of evil, which include doubt, selfishness, and anything that would intrude to harm ceremonies they were doing. Like most Zuni, this Clan Chief was a member of the Roman Catholic Church, and it could be said that he derived his position from that source — except that would not explain why the form of the War God, which preceded white intrusion, has always been exactly as it was — large figure, and tied to it the small figure and the four sticks.

I, of course, was delighted, and sat back to draw a deep breath, for it seemed like I had forgotten to breathe during the entire rite. Finally, I asked, "And when you do this in preparation to cure or heal — ?"

He did not allow me to finish the question. "Then," he said, "instead of many people, I see just the one I am treating. But when I am alone here I do it to get ready to serve all people — red, black, white, brown and yellow."

"Can anyone become a little hollow bone for *Wakan-Tanka* to work in and through?" I asked.

"Perhaps not a holy or medicine person, because we are called to that. But everyone can become a bone to serve others. And when they do they will find that in an emergency they can accomplish anything in half the time it would ordinarily take. They can also get immediately ready to work great things. If I do not have time to do anything else before I treat someone, I at least do this, because if necessary I can even do it in my mind."

"Where the bone idea is concerned, what is the difference between a holy or medicine person and an ordinary person?"

"The cleanest bones serve *Wakan-Tanka* and the Helpers the best, and medicine and holy people work the hardest to become clean. The cleaner the bone, the more water you can pour through it, and the faster it will run. It is this way with us and power, and the holy person is the one who becomes the cleanest of all."

Later on, while we were sitting in front of Fools Crow's house, we talked about the medicine men at Pine Ridge, Rosebud, and the other Sioux reservations; and it was now that we had our first conversation about how to tell an authentic medicine person from an imitation one. After this, other discussions were held on the same topic, until at last I had assembled all of his thoughts regarding the subject. These are combined in the following pages. Each of them was offered during a "palms up" moment, and I suspect that medicine people, both authentic and imitation, will find this information to be of considerable interest.[7]

"How does a Sioux become a medicine person?" I asked.

"Some people think we are chosen for this while we are still in our mother's womb. That might be so, because most of us start to become one when we are still a child. We have strange feelings about it, and we think about the Higher Powers more than other children do. We play games less, and do other things less. We go apart and contemplate what is happening to us. Of course, all of this is *Wakan-Tanka's* doing. He looks into us and sees what we are like. What is really happening is that He and *Tunkashila* are calling us.[8] What happens then is that we become more and more open to the Higher Powers. It is like we have bodies that are covered with holes through which they enter and fill us, and out of which our prayers and desires go up to Them. We are also ready to forego many of the ordinary pleasures of life so that we can become medicine people. We know that we must take the time needed to learn how to apply the power we will get for curing, healing, and helping our people in every way

---

[7] On pages 53 and 54 of the *Fools Crow* book, he lists the names of the outstanding ceremonial chiefs and holy men of the Western Sioux.

[8] Unlike most other Lakota holy and medicine men, Fools Crow did not think of *Wakan-Tanka* and *Tunkashila* as one and the same. They were one in mind and spirit, but individual Persons. When he defined their roles, he saw *Wakan-Tanka* as akin to the Father figure of the Bible, and *Tunkashila* as akin to the Son, Jesus Christ. "Why," he asked, "would we have two names for the same person, and why is it that our stories of our beginnings talk about a person like *Tunkashila* coming to our land long ago and walking about among us? No one ever says that this person was *Wakan-Tanka*. That is why, when I pray with my pipe, I point it first to *Wakan-Tanka*, then to *Tunkashila*, then to the Four Directions, and finally to Grandmother Earth."

that we can. As all of this happens, we are being changed (transformed), so that day by day we move deeper and deeper into what we are becoming. Doing this does not take away our regular responsibilities. We continue to share in the work that has to be done at home, and we must make our contributions to the needs of our communities. In fact, medicine people do what they do for their communities and nation. We are called to become hollow bones for our people and anyone else we can help, and we are not supposed to seek power for our personal use and honor. What we bones really become is the pipeline that connects *Wakan-Tanka*, the Helpers, and the community together. This tells us the direction our curing and healing work must follow and establishes the kind of life we must lead. It also keeps us working at things that do not bring us much income. So we have to be strong and committed to stick with this, otherwise we will get very little spiritual power, and we will probably give up the curing and healing work. The lessons we are taught by our human teachers, as Stirrup was for me, stress that the traditional way of performing a ritual is more important than curing someone. Curing a single individual is only important in terms of what this teaches the entire community. The community must continue to know that *Wakan-Tanka* and the Helpers are always with it, and that it need not be afraid. Seeing a person healed gives them this assurance, and it gives the community strength to carry on in the face of distress and disasters. So the medicine person sits at the center of every important thing that goes on in their community and nation, and when power is set in motion and distributed, it brings us more and even greater power. We emphasize that prevention is more important than treatment where the community and individuals are concerned. Getting ready in advance may not prevent our being hurt, but it keeps us from being destroyed. It is unfortunate, but our people have begun to forget this, and they are paying a tragic price for it. They get knocked down, and they do not have the strength or the way to get up.

"How," I asked, "does the difference between holy persons and medicine persons come into being?"

"Power takes over a holy person's life. It affects everything about us. So our knowledge and understanding increases faster, and before long our relationship to the Higher Powers and to power itself is different from that of medicine people. Also, holy men and women have more ways to obtain power and to set it into motion. We can heal others and ourselves more easily and quickly. We achieve peaks more often and our experience of them is deeper and more intense. Holy people can make spirit-travel trips to the dwelling places of the Higher Powers, and we can be transformed into animal or bird creatures who can go among people to see what is going on. It is holy people who are called upon by people and communities when situations are the most serious, and it is holy people who achieve the most impressive results. That is why there are only a few of us at any one time, and why we are the ones who can show people the fullness of power in motion. So we are called holy men or holy women. But all medicine people are different from ordinary people. They may, for the most part, behave and look like everyone else, but they are not. The way they think is different. What happens to them is different. They have insights that other people do not have. And, it is these thoughts and insights that enable them to reach the peaks that are required for their work. Another thing is that when we are compared to people who do not cure or heal, and even to medicine people, we are more emotional. This enables us to reach the peaks more easily and quickly. Because of our emotions, when we do a ritual or treat a person we can quickly change our intensity as we move toward a climax.

"Another thing we holy people know is who we are. We have a clear self-image. To say this is not bragging. It is the truth. We know we are part of Sioux history, and that when we have become hollow bones there is no limit to what the Higher Powers can do in and through us in spiritual things. Even our physical bodies cannot contain us, because our spirits can step out of our bodies and spirit-travel. We dream and vision and have fantastic thoughts. This begins while we are still children. Because of it, we are always ready for *Wakan-Tanka* and the Helpers to take us places and show us things that others, because of their having closed minds, may never see. The Power that we receive is for curing, healing, prophesying, solving problems, and finding lost people or objects. It is also for spreading love, transforming, and assuring peace and fertility. It is not to give us power over others because the source of power is not ourselves.

It comes to us and moves through us as hollow bones, but it belongs to *Wakan-Tanka* and the Helpers. They are the Source, and all thanks should go to Them.

"Still, the life of a holy person becomes soaked with power. One way to describe it is that we are like filled sponges. We think constantly about power, and the power we are given is easily set into motion. Our lives are a dance of power, and our people see this, so they honor us. It follows then that we are always in public view, and that our behavior must be the best. I do not argue, do not fight, do not hate, do not gossip, and I have never said a swear word. I have not chased after women, and I have controlled my lust for them. I have never touched a woman patient other than what was necessary to cure or heal them. I have not taken advantage of anyone. I have not charged for my curing, healing or advice, although I have accepted the gifts of gratitude people have brought to me. I have never touched alcohol or drugs; I have not even used peyote like they do in the Native American Church. *Wakan-Tanka* can take me higher than any drug ever could. Because of these things, and of my spiritual life, people respect me. But the important thing is that I reflect *Wakan-Tanka* and the Helpers to them. I am not Them, but people see what They are like in me and in the life I have lived. This life has been a very happy and a full one. I don't know how it could have been better. *Wakan-Tanka* did not tell me to forego the things I just mentioned. I just came to know that I would have a better life without them. One of the reasons why I have had such a hard time trying to find people to pass my medicine on to is that there are so few who want to live morally and frugally. While they talk a lot about wanting to do this, they do not really want to give up pleasure and material things. Also, you can tell a true medicine person from an imitator by what they ask you for in return for their help. According to where they live, everyone needs enough to live on and to pay their bills. But if they ask for more than a fair payment for this, walk away from them. They are only imitators, and their power will be very limited. They may talk well, and they may have created ceremonies that will charm you, but these will not be ceremonies that are traditional and that came from the Higher Powers. Remember that evil can work ceremonies too. The strongest protection we have against evil is our pipe. I use mine nearly every time I do a ceremony. The pipe is a sacred gift to the Sioux, and it represents for us the fellowship we have with *Wakan-Tanka* and the Helpers. When we have the pipe in our hands and use it in ceremonies it is the same as it would be for a Christian if he could hold Jesus Christ in his hands while he prays."

As previously stated, Fools Crow had told me that his entire work as a holy man, although demanding, was, "a dance of life," and he added that it was only when he did this dance that he was his true self. He was a vigorous and a charismatic man, and being with him was in itself a spiritual experience. Anyone who has been with him, Indian or outsider, will confirm this. I was told that the well-known actor, Robert DeNiro, went to see Fools Crow when the holy man was ninety-eight years old — and beyond carrying on any kind of a social conversation. The actor just sat with him for two days, but even then described it as one of the crowning experiences of his life.

What was accomplished in and through Fools Crow, did, of course, magnify his charisma. But he always stressed that both his power and the power that was added to his own was given to him for the sake of others. He considered this to be a normal view, and nothing unusual. If anything puzzled him about it, it was his inability to understand why everyone else did not feel the same way, and follow the same course of life that he did.

I asked Fools Crow whether he had any advice for those who felt they already had healing power, or were called to it.

"They must," he replied, "aim at the heavens and set themselves standards and goals that in the beginning will seem beyond reach. But they should enjoy the challenges this brings, and they should not look for perfection. One day they might get close to it. If, on the other hand, they aim low, that is where they will always be. Even failures make a positive contribution. They keep us humble, and they help us find and fix our mistakes. Failures also tell us to practice more until we are better. Things are never automatic in our relationship with *Wakan-Tanka*. He wants us to learn for ourselves what we are made of so that we can experience things fully. Quitting is the greatest failure of all. Don't. Put the work aside for awhile if you must, but then come back to it. It is practice that gives us confidence and gets us ready to meet the big tests when they come."

"How," I asked, "do you practice where curing is concerned? Wouldn't this be dangerous?"

He laughed, and answered, "I did my practicing in the early days on the little things — on small wounds and in situations that were not critical."

"I'm a little confused," I said. "If *Wakan-Tanka* and the Helpers tell you what to do, why is practice even necessary?"

Fools Crow grunted and sat up straighter. "While the power comes into and through us," he said, " it does not change the fact that we are human beings with limitations. The Higher Powers have to work with us as we are, even though we improve as time passes and we become less of a burden to them."

"Are there any basic rules for students to follow?"

"To become a clean hollow bone, you must first live as I have, or if you have not done this already, you must begin to do it. You must love everyone, put others first, be moral, keep your life in order, not do anything criminal, and have a good character. If you do not do these things, you will be easily tricked, and will become a hollow bone for the powers of evil. As I just said, you must also serve the Higher Powers for only what you should reasonably expect. If you demand more than this from the people you help, any power you receive will come from the evil ones and it will hurt what you are trying to do. Also, if people come to you just because they are curious and want you to perform some miracle for them, you should ignore them. *Wakan-Tanka* and the Helpers have better things to do than to satisfy the curiosity of unbelieving people. The greatest miracle is not something incredible, it is the thousands of changed lives. Miracles never make believers. A priest told me that one time Jesus fed five thousand men with a few fish and some bread. But when they came for breakfast the next morning, thinking they had found a restaurant where they didn't need to pay, he didn't feed them, and they all walked away. Miracles don't make believers."

"All of this has to do with faith," I commented.

"Ho," Fools Crow replied. "The one who wishes to be a true medicine person must be a person of faith, and they can only work successfully with those who also have faith. Good intentions are not enough, and excuses are not enough. The medicine person and the patient must be glued together in faith for the curing or healing to occur."

"Anything else?"

"Yes. The true medicine person and the holy person do not try to cheat, to just get by, or to fool anyone. Instead, they are the ones that always work and study the hardest. As long as we have the strength to do *Wakan-Tanka's* will, we work at our job constantly. Although we keep our lives in balance, we don't waste time. People can do anything if they want to do it badly enough. Of course, medicine persons must take the time to actually experience things to know how they truly are. Can we know how rain or snow feels without being out in it? Can we know how a Sun Dance feels without experiencing what a dancer does? Can we know about suffering if we don't suffer? Another thing medicine people need is a good sense of humor. You know that I enjoy life and like to laugh. Laughter breaks the tension. It is a very good healer. And, it keeps us from taking life too seriously. After all, *Wakan-Tanka* and the Helpers are the Chiefs of the ages. They have always been, and always will be. We come and go, but the sacred hoop was turning before us, and if we do what *Wakan-Tanka* wishes us to do, it will keep on turning after we are gone."

"Isn't it true though, that the holy and medicine people usually live longer than other people do?"

"There have been many medicine people with grey hair."

"How do you account for this?"

His eyes twinkled as they usually did when what he was about to say amused him, "I have been told," he said, "about the Fountain of Youth. But that is only a dream. If people really want to stay healthy and live a long time, there is a real way to do it. They must give themselves to *Wakan-Tanka* and live a spiritual life. They will have the peace that frees them from fear. They will know that *Wakan-Tanka* and the Helpers surround them, and that nothing can hurt them that they can't recover from. So there is no fear. They remain calm, and they are unhurried. They do not get ulcers or have sudden heart attacks while they are still young. I have had a couple, but I was eighty-five before I had the first one.[9] Spiritual people do not suffer as much from anxiety as other people do, and they do not worry as much about being chiefs or pleasing others just to get ahead in life. Instead, the things they do are personally rewarding. They feel good about themselves, and they naturally take care of themselves as they ought to."

"What you present," I said, "is an ideal picture, but is it realistic?"

"What," he asked, "does realistic mean?"

"Possible, probable . . . likely to happen."

He thought about that for a moment, and then answered me with another question. "Shouldn't we always remember that *Wakan-Tanka* does not ask us to do these things alone? He walks with us along the pathways of life, and He can do for us what we could never do on our own."

"Can you," I asked, "point to examples of longevity because of a spiritual life?"

"I am one," he said without the least indication of humility. "Black Elk is another . . . Charles Red Cloud is 89 . . . Iron Cloud and my father. There have been many I could name, and in fact I have named some of them for you (in the *Fools Crow* book). But I will admit that this is changing. Most of my people have begun to fall away from *Wakan-Tanka*, and with every passing day the examples get harder to find."[10]

---

[9] Reference to Fools Crow's illnesses can be found in *Fools Crow*, p. 201.

[10] I touch on the subject of longevity again in Chapter Four — The Timeless Age.

3 BONES IN ACTION

FOR ALL ANCIENT PEOPLES, EVERYTHING CONCERNING LIFE and death centers in power. One of the "nutshell" and easiest to understand concepts of power is that of the Kalahari Kung tribe of South Africa — portrayed by some writers as the most primitive tribe remaining in that country today, although others describe their culture as extraordinary and rich. They are still foragers, and represent a life-way that was followed twenty thousand years ago. The Kung believe that God, called Gao Na, implants at birth within the feet and ankles of each person a power, or energy, called "num." To stir up and set this power loose, they have a special healing dance which they perform to "dance it up." Even though everyone shares all of contemporary humanity's thought and behavior frailties, among those who are specially trained and attuned, num may continue to rise during the dance until it reaches a boiling point where it becomes "kia," which is a trance-like state of transcendence. Individuals achieving it become able to serve as channels for Gao Na to heal, prophesy, and make other valuable contributions to the villagers and visitors who are dancing with them.[11]

Fools Crow's understanding of power was similar to that of the Kung, although his articulation of it was different and certainly more comprehensive. In fact, his view is also different from that of some Native Americans and outside observers — although the accounts of Black Elk written by Neihardt and Brown make it clear that Black Elk and Fools Crow were in broad agreement about its nature and functioning. As for the idea of "boiling energy," we should recall that Fools Crow said, "When a person is right with God he always has a special feeling. When I am curing I feel a charge of power and I am excited! I know about these things because they are going on inside of me. When people come to me for help, for an ailment or curing or whatever, as I do my ceremony I feel the strength, the energy, building up. And I know I can cure them. The spirits let me know it. They even come inside of me and give me confidence and strength. And I feel good about this as it builds up inside of me."[12]

There is no consensus among Native Americans or outside observers regarding the definition of power, but their general view seems to be that power comes initially from a supernatural source or sources, and that it is best described as an astounding and electric-like energy that pervades the universe. Power is everywhere present and in varying degrees within everything. Some even play this out to where God becomes the sum of this energy. He exists in everything — so that it can justifiably be said that each of us is, in a sense, a part of God.

This was not Fools Crow's understanding of power.

Since, during the course of our conversations, he had used the word "power" many times, I asked him to explain what the word "power" meant to him.

It was another one of those areas he had taken for granted and needed no personal explanation for, so he had to struggle to formulate an answer. I knew that when it came it would have nothing to do with personal power as the outside world commonly thinks of it. Fools

---

[11] Katz, "Boiling Energy," 1982.
[12] *Fools Crow*, 1979, p. 207.

Crow cared little about status and position. He was not impressed by politicians, corporate executives, sports heroes, or film stars. After looking off into space for awhile he said, "At first, *Wakan-Tanka* had all of the spiritual power inside himself. But he loves to share things, so he gave some power to Grandmother Earth and some to each of the Persons he placed in the Cardinal Directions or mid-directions like southeast. Then He told them that when faithful human beings or other creatures called upon them for help they must send them their powers and save the people."

"I know," I said, "that some tribes, like the Hopi, were taught that the four Persons live in the mid-directions."

"Ho," Fools Crow replied, "*Wakan-Tanka* taught each tribe to believe in ways that work best for them. It depended on where they lived, and the way they thought about spiritual things."

"Your views," I said, "are shared by the medicine persons of many tribes."

"Once," Fools Crow responded, "I went to a Native American conference in Minneapolis. While I was there I visited with a medicine man from a Washington tribe. He lived two thousand miles from my country. But his God had taught his ancestors that He is the source of all power. This man was also taught that everything has a spirit. Even the rocks and the plants have a spirit. And he said that many white people don't know how to see this because they have no connection with the spirit forces of Grandmother Earth. All of these are things I have been taught also."

"Is it right to say that spiritual power is everywhere present?" I asked.

"No. *Wakan Tanka, Tunkashila,* Grandmother Earth and the Persons in the Four Directions each have their own power. Power is not everywhere present, but it is where they are and so it surrounds us. It is above, below, and on all four sides. Also, some power was given to each thing in the universe when it was created — Sun, Moon, stars, rocks, animals, birds, fish, plants, people . . ."[13]

"Is power everywhere present in the air?"

"No," he answered as he formed a circle with his hands. "It just surrounds us."

At this point he took a stick and drew a small diagram on the ground to show me exactly what he meant by "surrounds."

"You used the expression 'some power,'" I said. "Does this mean that different amounts of power are given to each thing?"

"Whatever it needs for ordinary survival."

I noted the use of the word "ordinary" as opposed to "extraordinary," and pursued it further. "You have not led an ordinary life," I said. "How do you apply what you just said to your own experience?"

He was warming to the subject and his eyes twinkled as he leaned forward in his chair. "You are talking about human beings now," he said. "*Wakan-Tanka* puts natural power inside of each person when they are born. As they grow up they can use this power for good or bad. They can build big cities, big ships, airplanes, bombs and armies. They can invent all kinds of wonderful things like refrigerators, televisions and telephones. Anyone with education and talent can do these things whether they believe in *Wakan-Tanka* or not. This is a gift *Wakan-Tanka* gives freely to us."

(I note that he did not restrict the location of the power to the feet and ankles as the Kung do, indicating that he was taught the power we are given at birth is diffused throughout our minds and bodies, and that atheists and believers alike are given natural power.)

"How is power different for people who do believe in *Wakan-Tanka?*" I asked.

"Believing people can soar beyond ordinary life. They can do what the white people call 'miracles.' If they want to have some of the knowledge and abilities of *Wakan-Tanka, Tunkashila*, Grandmother

---

[13] Brown records Black Elk as saying that the Great Spirit (Wakan-Tanka) is within all things . . . trees, grasses, rivers, mountains, four-legged and winged peoples; but more importantly He is above all these things and peoples, *The Sacred Pipe*, p. XX. Fools Crow did not use the title "Great Spirit" for Wakan-Tanka. He preferred "The Highest and Most Holy One."

Earth and the Persons, they can call in spiritual power and add it to their own."

"Then there is an important difference between the powers that are related to secular life and those that are related to spiritual life," I replied.

"What is secular?" he asked.

"Life in the daily world as opposed to spiritual life."

He stroked his chin before he spoke. "There is natural power, and there is spiritual power, but in the old days my people did not separate daily life in the world from spiritual life. Everything was spiritual. We were soaked with it. It is only now that we see a difference. Our attitude was spiritual, and *Wakan-Tanka* and his Helpers were involved in everything we thought and did. This is the way it has continued to be with me and in the lives of other traditional people."

"Tell me how spiritual power works, and what exactly it is. How do you call it in? What happens when you do?"

"Apart from when it is being used in a ceremony, spiritual power is not in a person or in a ritual item so that we can say we are powerful or that a ritual or ritual item has power. We can never heal a patient and say, 'I did that, and you can thank me for it.'[14] It is the Higher Powers and their Helpers who do this in and through us. We are helpers too, but only as hollow bones they work through. Most people think that to do and build great things is what really counts, but the greatest and the only lasting privilege we have is that in spite of some of the things we think, say and do, the Powers and their Helpers are still willing to work through us. What could be greater than to be *Wakan-Tanka's* mind, eyes, ears, nose, mouth, arms, hands, legs, and feet here on earth?"

"How would you describe spiritual power? Can we call it energy or electricity?"

---

[14] Please bear in mind that while, for purposes of clarity, I use the word "patient" throughout most of the book, Fools Crow did not use it. He always referred to those who came to him by their name, or as the "person." They had identities, and he did not want them to feel he thought of them as numbers or in any impersonal way.

"Sometimes it feels like energy or electricity when it is moving in and through us. But spiritual power is really a distinctive kind of knowledge that is like the key that opens the door or the switch that starts the energy moving. It is that special insight that we need to break up a log jam of knowledge. Other people may have gathered up the same amount of information we have, but they can't get it moving. They go nowhere because they have not called in the power and have not been given the key or switch to turn it on."[15]

I understood what Fools Crow was saying . . . all of us have experiences where we have gathered together a body of information about something and then seem unable to do anything of value with it. We think about it, and think about it, and nothing happens. Then one day that "Ah ha!" instant comes when a light goes on and we see the way to go . . . everything takes off. So spiritual power is not an everywhere-present energy, it is the prime mover; those key insights that are given to us by *Wakan-Tanka* and his Helpers. How then do we obtain these insights? "What," I asked, "is involved in obtaining these switches or keys? What must we do?"

"First cleanse (purify) ourselves ritually with smoke or water, and then let *Wakan-Tanka* make us into clean bones to work in and through for the sake of others. You have seen pipes that are clogged with junk or mineral deposits. People are like that, except that the deposits are the things that we put in *Wakan-Tanka's* way when we ask him to help us."

"What kinds of things do we put in the way?"

"Doubt, guilt, reluctance, fear, selfishness, wanting to tell *Wakan-Tanka* how and when it ought to be done . . ."

"You say we must do this for the sake of others. What about doing it for our own sakes? Is it wrong to ask for help with personal needs?"

"Of course we will ask for personal help, but our reason must be that we want to be helped so that we can help others. There must

---

[15] Black Elk agrees again as we find him telling Neihardt, "It is from understanding that power comes; and the power in the ceremony was in understanding what it meant; for nothing can live well except in a manner that is suited to the way the sacred Power of the World lives and moves. *Black Elk Speaks*, Neihardt, 1979, p. 208.

be nothing selfish in this. *Wakan-Tanka's* wish is that we do for others, and we are taken care of when others do for us. It is a community approach that provides a strong and united group whose voice is louder and more likely to be heard by *Wakan-Tanka* and his Helpers than a single voice would be. This approach gives us more personal satisfaction than if we just try to help ourselves. I heard a song on the radio which included the words, 'I did it my way.' This is nothing to be proud of, and the person who follows that way of life can not be happy for very long. Those who live for one another learn that love is the bond of perfect unity. Perfect unity is when you put other people ahead of yourself. Then when they put you ahead of themselves, there is perfect love — perfect unity — and no one has to worry about equality any more. You have something much better. Besides, you can never have equality, because the person you want to be equal with is not standing still and waiting for you to catch up. By the time you get there he or she will be somewhere else."

"Calling in *Wakan-Tanka*, the Persons, or Grandmother Earth," I asked, "how exactly do you do this?"

"Come with me," he said, and then picked up a small cloth medicine bundle and a pint jar as he arose to lead the way toward the creek. When we reached it, he filled the jar with water. Then he used his pocket knife to cut a quarter-inch diameter willow branch, and trimmed it until it was about twelve inches long. He formed a small hoop with this and used a strip of bark to bind the overlapped ends together.

"This is not the only way I call in," he said. "I do it with my pipe, and at the Sun Dance with pieces of colored cloth. But when I am alone here at home or at Bear Butte or some other questing place, this is how I do it."

He got down on his knees on the grass and cleared a twelve-inch square spot of ground in front of him. He picked a handful of sage that was growing nearby, and covered the cleared space with it. At each corner he put down a piece of colored felt to represent the Persons at the Cardinal Directions. On this altar he placed the small cloth medicine bundle he was carrying, and opened it to reveal six buckskin pouches, each of which contained in powder form one of the six directional colors. There were also several small brushes —

which were peeled sticks whose ends were pointed. He sat down on the ground, glanced at me to make certain I was observing every detail carefully, then placed both hands in his lap; the right one holding the hoop, and the left cupped to receive the gifts he knew would be coming to him from *Wakan-Tanka* and the Helpers. He closed his eyes, and deep-breathed seven times to relax and prepare himself. I knew, because he had told me previously how to do this, that each time he breathed he was envisioning the air entering through his finger tips, tracking it up into his chest, holding it briefly, letting it go, tracking it down his abdomen, out his legs and feet, and exiting out his toes. By the end of the seventh breath he would be completely relaxed and rid of any distractions. It was a means of isolating himself from intruders and evil forces, as the Pueblo Indians do with pollen or white strings laid across entrance paths while ceremonies are going on in their villages.

The breathing done, he began to chant softly and his brow furrowed as he concentrated intently upon calling in *Wakan-Tanka* and the Helpers. Several minutes passed before he opened his eyes. Then he picked up one of the brushes, dipped it in water, and mixed it with the red powder. Using this, he daubed a small spot of red paint onto the small hoop. Next he took yellow, and daubed a small spot of yellow paint onto the hoop. I had expected that he would use all four Directional colors and blue and green also, but he did not.

He read my mind and held the hoop out toward me as he said, "I use the small hoop to get myself out of the way of *Wakan-Tanka* and the Helpers. Knowing what the powers are in each of the Directions, from a human point of view I would pick those that I think are the most closely related to my problem. But I do not have the wisdom of *Wakan-Tanka*. Only He and the Helpers know which of them is truly best to send in for each situation. So through the tiny hoop they tell me this by making the choices for me, and when I follow their guidance it is only a little while before I see why they chose the ones they did."

I took the hoop and examined it, but I still needed more information. "And how exactly," I asked, "did they go about choosing these Directions for you?"

"When I close my eyes and sing, I roll my eyes up a little and look at the inside of my forehead. A small black screen forms there, and when I concentrate upon it, it is not long before colors come streaking in. They come in different ways at different times. What Stirrup taught me is to remember either the first two colors I see, or the two that are the brightest. Then I am to paint these on my hoop as a guide to which of the Directions I am to call in to begin my quest for answers. *Wakan-Tanka* knows that having more than two colors to call in can be confusing. If I get a color other than those of the Directions, or for *Wakan-Tanka* or Mother Earth, that is my color, and I know I am supposed to look within myself and examine myself as part of reaching the solution."

"Is this the same as having a vision?"

"No. But it is what I call 'visioning.' I will tell you more about visioning later on."

"Does the power come the moment you paint the color on the hoop?"

"No. *Wakan-Tanka* and the Helpers do not personally come, but contact is made with them. You can say they have answered the telephone and are ready to talk to me. But the power only comes to me and goes into action when I begin to use the concentration tools, such as a medicine hoop or crystal, that *Wakan-Tanka* has given us. Each of the Higher Powers has its own animal or bird messenger, and after we have used each concentration tool, this messenger brings to us a basketful of gifts bearing answers."

"How does power travel. Does it come like light beams . . . a bird . . . ?"

"It comes to me through my pipe. The pipe is like a water hose that connects me to the Source. When I point the stem of my pipe toward a Person, He sends me his powers through it. For example, the powers of the Person of the South are birth, life and destiny. When I need to know more about these things to solve a problem or to reach a goal, he sends me information about birth, life and destiny. We talk about these things, and He shows me how they relate to my problem. Then he shows me what I need to do to set this information into motion. For people who do not have a pipe, the powers come through the air."

"In the outside world these days," I said, "people are talking a lot about what you call 'concentration tools,' but they use the words, 'focusing tools.' Do you mind if I call them that for readers who are used to the words?"

"That will be *waste* [good]," he replied.

"By 'concentration tools' you mean the ancient rituals and the individual ritual items that were given to your people in the beginning?"

"Thoughts too. Anything that helps us concentrate and draws us more and more into the talking that goes on with *Wakan-Tanka* and the Helpers is a concentrating tool."

"You mentioned getting the power into motion. Are you saying that it comes, but that even though you receive it, it doesn't go into action automatically?"

"Yes. Even though we receive power, it does not move on its own. Something more is required of us to set the power into motion. We must show our faith and commitment by doing the things the Higher Powers have taught us to do. We begin by letting the Powers know that we are willing to be their servants to others. We do this by questing. We make a questing place in the ancient way, and then use it to quest. As we do this, employing one thought or tool after another, we are walking the ancient pathways. Each thought or tool leads to the next until the goal of our quest has been achieved. I call this walking of the pathways our 'dance of life,' although actual dancing is only one part of it. The walking does not stop until we die. The important thing is to let *Wakan-Tanka* and the Helpers lead, and then to wait patiently for the answers. They do not always send the messengers with these gifts right away. Sometimes they need to help us get ready so that we will recognize the answers when they come, and will make the best use of them."

As I considered what Fools Crow had told me, it became clear that the dynamics of spiritual power were simply extraordinary. Rather than our becoming of no consequence in the servant role, every ability and quality that we have is added to and called into play. The utmost is made of us. Our self-esteem and sense of personal value rises to its highest plane, and then exceeds it!

Fools Crow received from Stirrup, Iron Cloud, and directly from *Wakan-Tanka* and the Helpers, a broad array of thoughts and tangible focusing tools to work with. He was given countless ways to do things, and had more than one way to accomplish any individual goal or solution. Hence in instances where other medicine people have failed, he always succeeded, and in the process he was never bored or un-challenged. He was also given numerous ways to store up power. Whenever he was alone, he was busy fueling, or "powering" up. At night, or between daily treatments for curing or healing, he did the rituals that filled him as a hollow bone, so that he was always ready to have power dispensed through him.[16]

To summarize the foregoing about power, Fools Crow was taught that while we are each given natural power at birth, we are also surrounded by spiritual, or supernatural, power — which is spiritual knowledge that includes the knowledge needed to obtain power and to set it into motion. All human beings are born with natural power, but if we wish to go beyond this and have accomplished in and through us such spiritual wonders as transcendence for curing and healing, freedom from fear, and fertility in all things, we must entrust ourselves to *Wakan-Tanka*, Grandmother Earth, and the Per-sons in the four Cardinal Directions, and then call in spiritual power from them. When we have made contact, we can ask Them to send to us their individual spiritual powers to be added to our natural powers. Following this, we receive the knowledge we need to under-stand what we have been given, including the ways we are to follow to set the power into motion.

The procedure for receiving power is first, purification; second, becoming a clean tube for the Higher Powers to work in; third, using

---

[16] To illustrate how consistent and universal this Native American approach has been, the Desert Cahuilla of California believed that all wisdom for soul loss or soul damage was God-given. He told the medicine persons what to do. It was different for each person who came to be healed. There was no fixed routine. Sometimes, herbs were used, sometimes sucking, sometimes massage. God told them where to blow the smoke, or where to brush with eagle feathers. Always, it was God who revealed the particular way to go about healing through the medicine person. Modesto and Mount, 1980, p. 49.

the focusing tools to walk the ancient pathways where we will find guidance and ways to achieve goals; and fourth, dispensing this power to others. As all of this is done, we enter a spiritual dance of life that continues as long as we live. We should bear in mind that ideally this dance is a reciprocal thing in which everyone participates, so that we serve one another. By this sharing everyone is cared for. It follows the pattern of the Sioux "Giveaway ritual," in which a person or family who is in mourning or wishes to express gratitude, gives away virtually everything they have to needy families in the community. While the consequence would seem to be that of leaving the donors with nothing, the opposite happens. The tradition continues with other families who hold giveaways that replenish whatever the first donor needs. The result is a bonded and interdependent community in which everyone knows their essential security is guaranteed. Giveaways are still held on the reservations, although they are not so universally practiced as they once were. Among traditionalists, the concept remains strong, and you will find it expressed where you would least expect it. When I was invited recently to spend an evening with the Native Americans at Leavenworth Prison, in Kansas, they told me that their greatest desire was for the warden to permit them to perform ritual giveaways. Since they had limited tangible goods, I can only assume they intended to give to one another in a ritual manner their encouragement and support. Fools Crow would be the first to applaud the idea.

Fools Crow's procedure for calling in the Directional Persons and their attributes . . . . .

1. Make a small, 3- or 4-inch diameter hoop using willow or some other wood, or twisted paper.

2. Do the deep breathing exercise to completely relax and prepare yourself.

3. Close your eyes and look up at the inside of your forehead, thinking of it as a blank screen. Make the screen as black as possible.

4. Concentrate intensely and watch the Directional colors that come swirling onto the screen. Pay particular attention to the two that are either the first two you see or are the most vivid. Paint these on the hoop. They are the Directions the Beings want you to call on.

* Note that black will come as a grey line

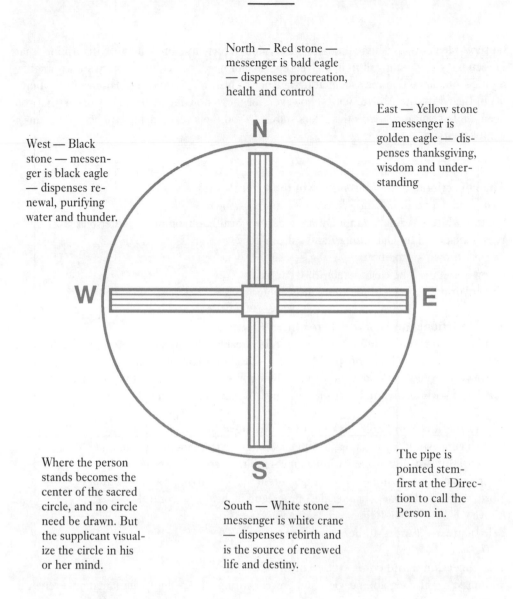

North — Red stone — messenger is bald eagle — dispenses procreation, health and control

East — Yellow stone — messenger is golden eagle — dispenses thanksgiving, wisdom and understanding

West — Black stone — messenger is black eagle — dispenses renewal, purifying water and thunder.

Where the person stands becomes the center of the sacred circle, and no circle need be drawn. But the supplicant visualize the circle in his or her mind.

South — White stone — messenger is white crane — dispenses rebirth and is the source of renewed life and destiny.

The pipe is pointed stem-first at the Direction to call the Person in.

5. Once the Directions he was to call upon were known, Fools Crow purified himself and used his pipe to call in the designated Persons and their attributes, or powers. These came immediately to him through the pipe, which served as a channel for this. He relaxed himself through closing his eyes and deep breathing to get himself into the fullest state of isolation and readiness for what was to come, sinking as far as was possible into an inky state of blackness. Once he was there, he let the Persons guide his thoughts about the powers they possessed, helping him to relate these to the questions or problems he was pursuing. He took ample time and did not hurry the process, waiting patiently for the answers to become clear. Then he gave a thank-offering.

Observe always that, when you use a black mind-screen and small hoop to determine what Directions you should call in in a given instance of need, the colors you are shown might mystify you, since that may seem at first glance to bear no significant relationship to your need. Bear with the Above Beings, however, for they know far better than you do what you need, and as you quest with the colors shown to you their relationship will become abundantly clear.

The Directional and color system of the Cherokees:
East - red - The Sun Land - success - triumph - power
South - white - Wa'hala' (a mountain) - peace - health - happiness - other blessings
West - black - The Darkening Land - death
North - brown - propitious
Below - green - The earth - rebirth - renewal
Underworld - yellow - about the same as blue

The Directional and color system of the Apache:
Southeast - turquoise blue - blue hoop - golden eagle - lifting off fear of retribution
Southwest - black - black hoop - black bear - lifting off fear of death
Northwest - yellow - yellow hoop - mountain lion - lifting off fear of not knowing
Northeast - white - white hoop - fox - lifting off fear of being impure

The Directional and color system of the Western Sioux:
East - yellow stone - golden eagle - thanksgiving - wisdom - understanding
South - white - white stone - white crane - rebirth - source of renewed life & destiny
West - black - black stone - black eagle - renewal - purifying water & Thunder
North - read red stone - bald eagle - procreation - health & control
Above - blue - Above Beings
Below- green - Earth Mother

The Directional and color system of the Cheyenne:
Southeast - white - golden eagle - sun power- spring - life - light - illumination - renewal
Southwest -red - mouse - summer - innocence - growth - weather & Thunder
Northwest - yellow - brown bear- fall - introspection - perfection - beauty & harvest
Northeast - black - buffalo - winter - wisdom - death - disease - numbness

The Directional and color system of the Hopi:
Southeast - red - red corn - ancestors providing
Southwest - blue or green - blue-green corn youth & courtship
Northwest - yellow - yellow corn - mature adult - illumination
Northeast - white - white corn - protective medicine to insure long & venerable life

4 HARMONY

IN *THE INVISIBLE PYRAMID*, LOREN EISELEY WRITES, "BUT THESE
ancient word-flight specialists the poets have another skill that en-
hances their power beyond even the contemporary ability they have
always had to sway minds. They have, in addition, a preternatural
sensitivity to the backward and forward reaches of time. They probe
into life as far as, if not farther than, the molecular biologist does,
because they touch life itself and not its particulate structure."[17]

He could easily have been writing about the Native Americans,
for many of them have been poets — certainly the medicine people
were. Their songs, prayers, and prayer-formulas are expressed in
poetic form, and they also learned to live simultaneously in the past,
present, and future. I describe their time dimension as, "The Timeless Age," a name passed on to me by Philip Bruno, a personal friend
who thought of it first, because it is not bounded by one age or another.
In it, all ages merge. People are incorrect when they call Native
American traditions "New Age," for they are not. It just happens that

---

[17] Eiseley, Loren, *The Invisible Pyramid*, p. 125.

the things New Age people identify with have been done by the Native Americans for thousands of years, so there is a feeling of connectedness. Understandably then, New Age followers gravitate to Native American rituals and ritual thought, although for the most part the reverse is not true.

Also, Native American traditional life cannot be constrained by the bounds of Old Age, for although the rituals remain constant, and power is set in motion when they are done in the traditional way, the Native Americans, as they look at things through the eyes of the Higher Powers, are enabled to see how to use the hallowed rituals in association with present day needs.[18]

So the past is constantly linked to the present, and both of these are linked to the future in that they are future oriented and make the future possible. They cause the people to think in terms of providing for it. Whenever the hoop is drawn, or a ritual takes place in a circle, all three ages are included within it.

Fools Crow said to me, "Our children are us in the tomorrow of life. In them we remain here, and so it will be with their children's children — if the world survives."

"Does this idea go farther than a linkage of ages?" I asked.

"The linkage of ages has taught us to think in terms of the linkages of many things. Mind, body and spirit are linked together. You cannot consider one without the others. The Higher Powers, the medicine person, and the community are linked together. People, other creatures, and the rest of creation are linked together. Thinking in dimensions like these keeps us from being narrow and self-centered. Instead, it stretches and expands the mind."

It was clear that Fools Crow understood the need for these concepts better than most people, and he said so clearly in his four-part prayer of thanksgiving, which he made when he deposited food

---

[18] From a Christian point of view, what Fools Crow claims about looking at things through God's eyes is not far-fetched. Paul wrote to the Ephesians, "But God, who is rich in mercy, out of the great love with which he loved us, even when we were dead through our trespasses, made us alive together with Christ (by grace you have been saved), and raised us up with him, and made us sit with him in the heavenly places in Christ Jesus, that in the coming ages he might show the immeasurable riches of his grace in kindness toward us in Christ Jesus." Ephesians, Ch 2, v. 4-7.

in the ground after meals, whenever he concluded a ritual, at curings or healings, and at the end of every personal prayer session. The verses of the prayer were usually sung, although he sometimes did it silently, but it was not in either instance like his other songs, for it was done frequently and the words changed a little from song to song. In general though, it went as follows:

"*Wakan-Tanka*, I thank you for our ancestors — for the life they have given each of us, and for the traditions they preserved and handed down to us.

"*Wakan-Tanka*, I thank you for my life and the opportunity it has given me to know you, to serve you, and to serve our people. Continue to make me a responsible person, and help me add to the good things You and my ancestors have given me.

"*Wakan-Tanka*, I thank you for those who are yet to come, and who will carry on from where we leave off. Help them preserve the traditional life for the generation to come after them, and so keep the hoop turning.

"Finally, *Wakan-Tanka*, I thank you for my friends who are here with me to share this precious moment. I pray that you will bless them and always be with them."

What I have just written about the Timeless Age was not something said by Fools Crow during a "hands up" time, but where he is concerned it is something I have not covered before. I do so now because I saw in his life what results from this profound attitude — the sense of unity and brotherhood it brings into being, and how this awareness expands to embrace the whole of creation, so that each part of it becomes a living "brother" or "sister." It reaches out to embrace environment and ecology, and it is the core ingredient of harmony in the world.

I have seen this same unity expressed by the Apache when they form groups and link arms to dance in concert and unity with the pubescent girl at her Sunrise Ceremony.

I have seen the Cherokees express it at their present day stomp dances, when at a certain point they form a single line, one behind the other, and then dance as they all reach forward for just a moment and gently lay their hands on the shoulders of the people in front of them.

Fools Crow expressed it in his everyday life. And, his attitude about interconnectedness was another way in which he was given a deep sense of belonging, place, contentment, and peace — the latter being defined by him as, "freedom from fear." Only those Native Americans who have forfeited their cultural attachments have no sense of place or center. The traditionalists have these things, and it gives them an inner harmony that increases their longevity. Fools Crow lived to be ninety-nine. Black Elk lived to be ninety. Fools Crow's father, Eagle Bear, was ninety-eight when he died. Even at the turn of the century, when life expectancies the world over were far shorter than they are now, Densmore's medicine men informants were all in their sixties and above.

"Is there a way," I asked Fools Crow, "that *Wakan-Tanka* has given you to focus your mind upon your relationship with the rest of creation?"

Now his palms were up. "Becoming," he answered.

"How do you do this?"

"Stirrup taught me to hold an object in my hand and become it. If it is too big to hold in my hands, then I hold it in my heart."

I waited while he bent down and picked up a small, grey rock. He held it in his open palm and scrutinized it as he continued to speak. "*Wakan-Tanka* and Grandmother Earth have given all things life. This includes rocks, trees, water, and the ground we walk on. And just as people, animals, birds, bugs and sea creatures have blood in them, so too everything else has thoughts, feelings, concerns and hopes."

"What do you do," I asked, "to become something like a rock?"

"I talk to it like I do to a person, and I let the rock talk to me. It tells me where it comes from, what it has seen, what it has heard, and what it feels. We become friends. When we are finished, I have a whole new picture of that rock. Doing this expands the way I behave toward rocks and toward other things, and my mind grows. The more I do 'becoming,' the wiser I become about everything."

Later on, I would learn that Fools Crow carried the practice of "becoming" even farther. Whenever he was doing a ritual, he would

pick up some item he was using and press it to his chest. When I asked why he did this, he said he was becoming that item and identifying with it in order to experience it and understand it completely. Beyond the obvious implications of the gesture, what excited me was knowing that establishing such a relationship was the core principal of Navajo curings with sand paintings. As the Navajo medicine man, called a "singer," presses different portions of the painting to the patient's body, the patient identifies with the powers it represents and is given a heightened sense of the life and longevity that attends the supernatural world. In other words, because the patient believes this, longevity is transferred to him, and it has a profound effect upon his self-healing system.

"Do you believe that a rock or earth has feelings?"

"If everything that has been created is essential to life and balance and harmony, then they do. It depends upon how you think and how you define life. If you believe something has life, it has life. *Wakan-Tanka* has taught us to think about creation this way, and when we do, the life all things have within them becomes apparent to us, and we treat them accordingly. We do not abuse or misuse them. It is one thing to step on something you think has no life or feelings, and another to step on it when you think it does. When I pray each day, I pray for the health and healing of the whole creation, not just for people. And I ask *Wakan-Tanka* and the Helpers to help me walk on Grandmother Earth with compassion and understanding for all that exists."[19]

"Do you step on ants?"

"Not if I can help it. Sometimes when I am out walking, I don't see them until I have stepped on some."

"What if they come into your house and are after your food?"

"I put some of the food out for them in another place and try to lead them away."

"And if they ignore this bait and keep coming?"

"*Wakan-Tanka* does not give us the right to overcome other creatures, and they do not have the right to overcome us."

"Then you kill some?"

"I do what I must to get them out of the house."

"I have read," I said, "that without ants, the rest of creation would be in bad trouble."

"This is true, of everything," Fools Crow said as he shook his head up and down. "Something I have not mentioned where other creatures are concerned is that they do what they do naturally. We do what we do by choice. Animals and birds kill because that is natural

---

[19] All Pueblo Indian rituals are done for the sake of the entire world, not just for the sake of the Pueblo people themselves.

for them. We do most of our killing not because we need to, but because we want to."

As I thought about Fools Crow's remarks, it reminded me of Albert Schweitzer's "reverence for life." I've never known whether he meant we should reverence all living things, or that human life itself depends on how we treat other life. Perhaps both ideas were involved. However it was, Fools Crow went further than Schweitzer did, since he believed that our reverence should be for the whole of creation, including both the animate and the inanimate.

"Are you aware of the terrible environmental problems that are plaguing the world today?" I asked.

"People tell me about them, and I see pollution and waste wherever I go. Even my own people have left their ancient ways to join in this disaster now."

"Is it possible to heal the world?"

"With *Wakan-Tanka*, everything is possible. Without Him, it is not. Human nature, which is natural power without the added spiritual power that surrounds us, is such that people do not do what is for their own best good." [20]

"If it could happen, how and where would it begin?"

"With self-healing. People must let *Wakan-Tanka* and the Helpers heal them first so they will know how healing works. Then this understanding can be sent out from them to the rest of creation. Long ago, people knew how to do it, but they have forgotten the way. We can be hollow bones for healing the world, just as we can be bones for curing, healing, and helping one another."

"Does all of the fault for the present situation lie with human beings?"

"Only human beings have the power to unbalance the earth, and when they unbalance the earth they unbalance themselves. It is like that thing the Australian natives throw that comes back at them [the

---

[20] In the *Fools Crow* book, we are given his view regarding the coming of the end times, which he said he had been told was close upon us. Nevertheless, he also believed that this cataclysmic end could be delayed by a change in world belief and behavior, and also by a fair settlement of the Sioux claim against the United States Government for the Black Hills. pp. 195-196.

boomerang]. *Wakan-Tanka* made the earth so that it does everything to take care of itself. Everything fulfills its role — ants, worms, vultures, wolves, pebbles, sand . . . when we damage any of these or the earth itself, we damage ourselves. We cannot use them up or waste and destroy them without paying a terrible price for it. But people are doing this, and it is coming back on us all. Grandmother Earth is crying out about it. She is shaking the land [earthquakes] more and more to tell us how she feels, and to get our attention. *Wakan-Tanka* has told me that the Thunder Being will be sending great floods to show us the great cleansing that needs to go on within people. Our children will cry more than we will for this, and during our visits *Wakan-Tanka* has told me that their crying will be long and very loud."

"You have said that *Wakan-Tanka* does not punish us. How then do you think of natural disasters as something that teaches us lessons? Do you think that if we all believed and prayed, there would be no more earthquakes or floods?"

Fools Crow did not like my question, and I could see in his face that he was toying with the idea of not answering it. For a moment, I found myself wondering whether he had thought his position through. I was wrong. All he needed was time. "In the Garden of Eden, there were no earthquakes," he said, "but *Wakan-Tanka* changed all of that. Since then natural disasters have always happened."

"So what does that tell us?"

"Don't build your tipi in a creek bed or on the side of a volcano!"

As we continued to discuss the matter of power in terms of something given to everyone, Fools Crow made it clear that without the addition of spiritual power man's tendency is to use his natural power for himself, and while he accomplishes outstanding things on the earthly plane he nevertheless tends to subordinate and misuse the rest of creation; until, of course, he at last sees that he created a monster that has turned and will soon devour him. The Higher Powers teach the person with appended spiritual power not to do this.

The truth of Fools Crow's belief is plainly before us today as we experience the consequences of misuse. They threaten us, encompass us, and are in our very midst.[21] When the first Earth Day was held twenty years ago, the scientist Barry Commoner alerted us to the hideous environmental costs of our technological development. In his recent book, *Making Peace With the Planet,* he reviews the vast efforts made to control the damage and shows us why, despite billions of dollars spent to save the environment, we now find ourselves in a more perilous moment than ever — "environmental pollution" he declares, "is an incurable disease." Where once it seemed we really could save the earth by recycling, controlling, and solar energy, and it seemed that a revolution was afoot, we have fallen far short. Attempts have been halfhearted, the government has made terrible miscalculations, and private industry has deliberately resisted change.

The shortcomings Commoner refers to continue, and the fact that we even needed to have an Earth Day in the United States on April 22, 1990, and an International Earth Day on June 5, 1990, is an embarrassing testimony to our failure. As for Earth Day and what it actually accomplished, the jury will be out for some time. It appears that individuals and private industry are picking up the torch. One of the most heartening evidences of this is the recent international agreement to banish by century's end the manufacture of fluorocarbons that play a major role in the depletion of the ozone layer. Also, a high percentage of citizens in the United States, and I assume in Europe, are recycling goods and boycotting manufacturers of packages and products that are environmental hazards.

But monumental and ongoing action will be needed before the true measure of response is known. Some of the televised commentaries of Earth Day stick in the mind — like the groups of young people in Los Angeles who openly admitted that the only reason they

---

[21] The environment is getting plenty of press today, but for penetrating reading I suggest the following classics: Commoner, Barry, *Making Peace With the Planet;* Carson, Rachel, *Silent Spring;* Gribbin, John, *Hothouse Earth;* and Schell, Jonathan, *The Fate of the Earth.* Full data regarding these can be found in the bibliography.

attended the rallies was to see the guest stars who came to perform, and like the sobering images of strewn litter covering the ground after the crowds had gone home. Listening to a recent news report, I learned that in 1989 alone, four thousand tons of debris, most of it plastics, were picked up on the beaches of Los Angeles. What, do you suppose, was the world's total? Along with this the reporter cited a litany of tragedies among wildlife that were eating or caught in the plastics — such as the rings that hold six-packs together. Good intentions are all too often shallow and short-lived — even when the situation being addressed is one that could end life itself. At one time, the threat of a nuclear holocaust hung over us all. Its presence has by no means disappeared, but with the dramatic political changes in Europe, and with the melting of the cold war between the United States and the Soviet Union, we are freed to see perhaps an even greater ogre in the environmental threat. Because of its global dimensions, this threat may prove to be worse than a nuclear war. Also, while the nuclear peril just sits there, the eco-ogre is eating away at us every moment. It never stops. One report states that, even if production ceased today on everything that has damaged the ozone layer, it will take hundreds of years to repair the harm that has already been done. Paralleling this problem, there is the rapid destruction of the biologically rich tropical forests in South America, Africa, and Asia, which is causing a mass extinction of animal species, and of plants whose pharmaceutical value is inestimable. Edward O. Wilson, professor of biology at Harvard and one of the world's leading experts on biological diversity, estimates that four thousand to six thousand species are being lost each year as a result of deforestation, an estimate he says is very conservative. There is a pressing need to find and classify plant and animal species in tropical forests before forests and species disappear. Brazil's Atlantic forest is estimated to cover only one percent to five percent of its original area, and that nation's Amazon forest also is being cleared at a rapid rate.

Commoner's answer is to fundamentally redesign the way we produce goods, and to have community organizations play key roles in scrutinizing and directing environmental action — with all issues being dealt with simultaneously and together. But the cost of this would be monumental, while Fools Crow's solution would require relatively little funding, and in the end be more effective — first because it is based upon the proven traditional Native American approach that required no funding at all, and second because it has the power and potential to reach every person in the world now and in the future. It is to fundamentally change the attitude of every person toward the whole of creation . . . to bring people back in this respect to where the Indians were before European intrusion. It centers in education and attitude, reaching immediately out to adults, and with children being taught by parents and schools from the earliest possible age on that everything in creation is alive, makes its particular contribution, and has special value. Basic to this is the Native American understanding that humankind is not superior to the rest of creation and has no inalienable or God-given right to dominate or abuse it. Instead, we are only one part of a giant web whose assemblage of strands, with its strands working cooperatively together, is what accounts for its overall strength. In this respect, each strand is responsible to and for the rest. When we fail to carry our share of the load or when we abuse or destroy another part, it injures, sometimes irretrievably, all of the others, and often unbalances life in totally unexpected ways. Rachel Carson placed this grim specter before us in *Silent Spring,* when she spelled out in searing paragraph after paragraph how, while no responsible person contends that insect-bore disease should be ignored, "The question that has now urgently presented itself is whether it is either wise or responsible to attack the problem by methods that are rapidly making it worse. The world has heard much of the triumphant war against disease through the control of insect vectors of infection, but it has heard little of the other side of the story — the defeats, the short-lived triumphs that now strongly support the alarming view that the insect enemy has been made actually stronger by our efforts. Even worse, we may have destroyed our very means of fighting."[22]

As I write this, I cannot help thinking that such rare and incisive understandings as Fools Crow's came to a man who could only read English with great difficulty. He did not read books, magazines, or

---

[22] Carson, 1962, p. 266.

newspapers, and he did not have a personal television. The latter was a luxury he shared, often with misgivings, at someone else's home, in a motel, or in some public place. He did not attend public schools. He told people he did not speak English, but what he meant was that he did not speak it fluently. When Dallas Chief Eagle was not present, and Fools Crow and I were alone, he could speak English well enough that with some prompting from me an effective conversation could be carried on. And, he certainly understood English. His vocabulary was limited, and he would turn to me for definitions of certain words, but he always had a clear sense of what was being said. Over the years, he learned enough to handle things quite well — as any politician who tried to lead him astray quickly found out.

On this basis alone, it would be fair to describe him as an uneducated man. But he traveled far in his younger years, including to Canada, Europe, and to New York City, and some in his later years, including to Washington, D.C. He was a guest on television and radio shows. He also had an unusual ability to quickly soak up and analyze what he saw and heard. Other Lakotas and non-Indian friends kept him fairly well informed about events in general, and especially about what was going on at the Sioux reservations. He attended tribal meetings, held councils, and went to inter-tribal conferences. At intervals he had a radio, although never for long since someone always took them and sold them. But the wisdom that truly mattered, he would tell you, came from the Higher Powers — sometimes directly and sometimes indirectly. Considering what he accomplished, I find that assertion hard to contest.

What educational technique of his can we use to begin the re-thinking and the reawakening? I was with Fools Crow one morning when he went, as he often did, to speak to a class of children in a local elementary school. When he finished his talk — which was about heritage, morality, education and responsibility — the children were released for recess. As Fools Crow and I walked across the playground toward my car, more than a dozen of the boys and girls gathered around "grandpa," and tugged on his trousers to stop him. "Teach us," they said, and promptly sat down at his feet. It was evident that they had done this before.

He smiled at them as he picked up a small rock and held it out to them in the palm of his hand. "Talk to the children," he said to the stone in Lakota. And then, in a falsetto voice and in ventriloquist fashion he proceeded in a mixture of Lakota and English to draw out for them the life in the rock. Its name, it seemed, was "Swift Eagle," and he solemnly introduced it to each of the children. Swift Eagle had all kinds of things to say to them about what he had seen over the centuries, and what he thought about all of this — especially about the days when the buffalo were thick on the Great Plains and the Sioux followed the herds. Before long, thirty rapt children had gathered at his feet. Recess and playtime were forgotten, and not one of them wanted to return to class when the bell rang.

But Fools Crow waved good-bye to them, and we continued our walk to the car. As we reached it, Fools Crow turned to me and said, "I wish our teenagers would listen like that. But they just don't care anymore. Their future seems too bleak, and they think that trying to change it isn't worth the effort."

Nevertheless, "becoming" is a delightful way to introduce children to the idea of, and need for, living in harmony with the rest of creation. It works well with adults too for that matter; I've done a lot of successful "becoming" with them.[23]

---

[23] See *Fools Crow*, pp. 197-198, for more information about Fools Crow's view regarding the problems facing the Sioux reservations.

5 MIND SCREENS

WE WERE TALKING ONE AFTERNOON ABOUT THE WISDOM EX-hibited by the medicine and holy people of the Native American tribes when I asked, "Frank, how do you know all of the wonderful things you do? Have you been given insights that others haven't?"

He held up both hands, palms forward. I switched off the tape recorder, and picked up my note pad. I needn't have hurried though, since he blinked several times, rubbed his hands together, and squirmed a little as he looked at me. Several minutes passed before he spoke. I knew why he was doing this — he disliked the idea of anyone thinking of him as someone special.

Finally then, he began: "I have not been given anything that others can't have. My ancestors were all taught how to have sacred dreams. In these dreams all kinds of strange and beautiful things would happen, things that never could take place in ordinary life. Strange beings would appear and every kind of creature would come in awesome forms. These visitors would speak to the people and give them messages. They learned who their helpers would be, what *Wakan-Tanka* wanted them to do, and how He would help them do it. They also learned, and perhaps this was the most important thing, how to look at things through the eyes of the Higher Powers. The medicine people had the greatest of these dreams. Theirs were the most awesome, the most powerful, and sometimes the most frightening."

"Why do you think the medicine people's dreams have been more powerful than those of other people?"

"As I have already told you but will say again, they have been individuals whose natures and way of life opened them fully to *Wakan-Tanka* and the Helpers. There was something else special about the medicine people. Most of their medicine dreams did not seem to be dreams to them. They seemed to be things that really happened, since they were often not asleep when the dreams took place. We know this because the stories of these dreams were passed down, and some of them were told to white people who put them in books. I have heard the stories from elders, and friends have read a few of the accounts to me. Some of my own visions and dreams really happened to me, so I can say that I really did this or that, no matter how unusual the events were. There is, though, one thing that has not been told to outsiders, which is the way many of these dreams actually happen."

His concluding remark moved me forward to the edge of my chair. I sensed that I was about to learn something that was extremely special. "And this gift of dreaming," I said, "is what accounts for your surpassing insights?"

"Not all, but most of them. And I should tell you that I call my dreaming by another name. I call it, 'visioning,' and I will tell you how it is done. *Wakan-Tanka* and the Helpers taught me how to see with my mind, touch with my eyes, and decide with my heart."

Beautiful, I thought! And as I learned about visioning I gained the true feel of the Old Lord of the Holy Men in all of his sensitivity and love. "Why," I asked, "do you see with your mind rather than your eyes?"

"Because," he answered, "the mind can see farther than the physical eye. It can see what a camera can't see. It can see beyond physical barriers and even into a person. The mind's eye changes the way we judge things."

"How?"

"When we see with our mind we do not judge people or situations by their appearances. A person might not be beautiful on the outside, but will be a beautiful person on the inside. And when we serve as bones for *Wakan-Tanka* and the Helpers, we learn to see things in a new and magical light, to look at people and situations in different ways. Visioning is learning to let the Powers show you things through their eyes. People deny themselves wonders by failing to recognize that this can happen."

"Where did you learn about this kind of visioning?"

"Iron Cloud taught me how to do it, and my father, Eagle Bear, also knew how."

"In what way," I asked, "does looking through the eyes of the Higher Powers change things for you?"

"They are not limited as we are. They see the past, present, and future as one. They also know what is going on in people's minds and hearts, and they know what following a certain pathway will lead to. When we pray and listen, when we are using concentration tools, the Higher Powers can show us these things, and increase our wisdom."

"Can you give me some examples of what happens when you do this 'looking?' "

"*Wakan-Tanka* and the Helpers cast spiritual light onto things so that I can see them for what they really are. You will notice how the sun does this to the earth during the day, and how things look different in different light. That is what the Higher Powers do for me in spiritual matters. This light also pushes the darkness away and shows me what is there. It helps me walk around things and see them from different points of view — front, back and both sides. I see new colors and I feel what is going on around me. Then I close my eyes and wait for the images to form on my mind-screen. I continue to do this until all of the information comes together in a way I can use it. Then I concentrate even harder until the final picture is stuck firmly in my memory. Sometimes I cry because of the great beauty of it all. Ordinary things become extraordinary. What is nothing to someone else becomes marvelous to me and an exciting way to go."

"It sounds like *Wakan-Tanka* and the Helpers stretch and fill your mind in spectacular ways through visioning," I said.

"*Wakan-Tanka* and the Helpers have helped me imagine things that can not be seen by the physical eye. I can feel and see things most others miss. Pictures come into my mind, and soon I can find new approaches and ways to change everything around me. This is very helpful when I am curing or healing. When I am alone at night or between treatments, one of the things I do is visioning. Through it, *Wakan-Tanka* and the Helpers enable me to overcome obstacles that the illness or evil powers are raising up. And They tell me different ways to go to overcome these. By this, what would otherwise be impossible becomes possible."

"You know," I said, "it's as though They reverse things for you mentally."

"They show me how to see things from different points of view, to see how this way or that way might work in each situation. As I turn this information over in my mind, I become more creative, more fertile. But I do not become too involved with little details — just the big picture."

"So," I said, "there is a lot of yourself in what you do."

"The fact that I am a little hollow bone does not mean that I have no importance where *Wakan-Tanka* and the Helpers are concerned. On the contrary, they give me every opportunity to use my natural talents and abilities. This is true for everyone who serves them. Twenty medicine men will treat a person in twenty slightly different ways, and this is one of the fascinating things about curing and healing. We all respond differently to *Wakan-Tanka,* and do what we do the way each of us hears and feels His guidance. I am telling you this for the book so you can tell others. In their personal relationship with the Higher Powers, people out there will use the concentration tools a little differently than I do. The first time they might try to copy me exactly, and maybe the next time. But then they will reshape what they do until it is entirely their own in communion with the Higher Powers. When the desired results are reached, they should not ask how it happened or whether it was done like I would do it. They should just accept it and be glad."

What Fools Crow was revealing caused me to shake my head in wonder before I continued. Then I asked, "You spoke of touching with your eyes. How do you do this?"

"I use my eyes to touch with gentleness and love. When I cry for someone, I am touching them with my eyes. You can tell a lot about a person by looking into their eyes, and you can say things to people with your eyes that you cannot say with words. Eyes betray truth or dishonesty. They tell me how a person really feels about me. Many illnesses can be seen in people's eyes when you know how to look. When I am curing or healing, I give my faith to the person by sending it to them through my eyes. We make contact, and if they don't have enough faith already, what they see in me as the days pass will become theirs. This is one of the ways I get their mind inside of my mind so that they can see what I am being shown by *Wakan-Tanka* and the Helpers. I already told you that this is the first thing I have to do to be successful in treating them."

"Is there more with the eyes?"

"Our eyes enable us to touch nature, and to learn from it as we watch the seasons, the different skies, the winds, the grass, the streams and lakes. We observe that a big lake is never still, while a little one serves as a mirror. Clouds are different shapes that resemble many things, and they are always changing. Our ancestors saw their first tipi in a cottonwood tree leaf. We apply these lessons to people and to how we should understand all things. Even squinting at something will change what we see in it. So too the way people sit, stand, walk, or dance can tell us many things about them. Over the years I have learned to see with my brain by understanding my inside [innermost] thoughts about *Wakan-Tanka* and people, then to feel with my eyes, and finally to let my heart tell me how to be fair, and which pathways to follow."

"Why do you decide with your heart and not with your mind?"

"If I decide with my mind I am influenced by all kinds of thoughts that fight against one another. If I try to decide with my eyes, even though I see with love, it is hard to not be influenced by what I actually see — how people look, react, and what they are doing. If I decide with my heart, my judgments are never harsh. My heart takes into account the things that have hurt people — what they have had to deal with just to stay sane and alive. I guess this can be applied to most of the people in the world. My heart thinks about fairness, comfort and hope. It is like *Wakan-Tanka's* heart, which accepts us as bones to work in and through even though none of us deserves this great honor."

I nodded as I remembered the time I was at his home and nine people were living there, using up his food, bedding, furniture and fire wood. Some of the men were drinking, and none of them contributed anything. As was often the case, they had simply moved in on him. I asked Fools Crow why he didn't boot them out. His answer was, "Kate would cry, and I couldn't stand that."

"You haven't mentioned ears, nose, and mouth," I pointed out. "Don't these play important roles in your visioning?"

"Yes, but not in the same way. When I do visioning with my mind, eyes, and heart, I see through the eyes of the Higher Powers and not as people with only natural power do. This is usually the reverse of what humans will see because we are influenced by our motives and desires."

"So then, how does the nose fit in?"

"Aside from the usual things a nose does, like breathing, it stirs up our memories, so it works like a treasure chest that connects us to the past. Smells are associated with everything we do. *Wakan-Tanka* has covered the earth with them, and we can combine many of them to produce more. The sweet ones, like sweetgrass and sage, are protective in that they turn evil away, since its only connection is with bitter things. So we wear sage in the Sun Dance to draw the Higher Powers close because they like sage, and to keep anything away that might harm what we are doing. Smells also cause us to feel, to want, and to invent. They provide an atmosphere of mystery and ancient things, and they stir up our emotions."

"And ears?" I asked.

"Everything that exists has a sound," he answered, "and when things pass close by one another there is even a sound between them. This is how music comes into being. *Wakan-Tanka,* Grandmother Earth, and the other Helpers use sounds to communicate to us — sometimes in words, but more often to stir up our minds and hearts to think of spiritual things. Grandmother Earth speaks to us through the drum. Rattles are the soft voice of *Wakan-Tanka* sending showers of blessings down to earth. Flutes are the many voices of the Persons in the Directions. Thunder is the powerful voice of the awesome cloud beings. It is the ears that rocks speak to first, and through the ears to the mind, spirit, and heart. All of the beautiful sounds that exist or come into being are *Wakan-Tanka's* creations, and like the other beautiful things he has made, he is a sucker for them. He can't resist coming closer when we use them. We know He is there and sharing the experience with us."

It can be seen that through visioning, without his having learned the biological manner in which the left and right brain work, Fools Crow was taught a life-way that drew naturally upon the right brain.

He went on to say that visioning was like opening a door, but a person must walk through the door to experience the wondrous things that are in the great and magical room on the other side. Even when we get there, he added, it is absolutely fundamental that we must "believe in order to see," rather than to follow the scientific approach of seeing in order to believe. "How else," Fools Crow asked, "can *Wakan-Tanka* and the Helpers show their wonders to us?"

Oh yes, about the mouth. "The mouth," Fools Crow said, "is what we taste with, eat with, and communicate with . . . but it is also what gets us into trouble!"

6 MENTAL MOVERS

IN HIS INITIAL VISION QUEST IN 1903, FOOLS CROW WAS GIVEN A certain powerful medicine and numerous ways to perform healing and curing rites. In subsequent vision quests *Wakan-Tanka* gave him powerful healing songs, and three of the most phenomenal meditation and focusing tools ever handed down to humankind. Along with his regular use of the Sun Dance, the Purifications Lodge, and the Yuwipi, his diligent employment of these songs and tools played the greatest roles in stirring up and setting loose the power that *Wakan-Tanka* and the Helpers had added to his own. One tool enabled him to do thought transference — conveying thoughts and instructions to other people, influencing them, and also learning what they were being told, thinking, and doing. A second tool empowered him with continual strength, longevity, and regeneration by giving him a wondrous way to achieve daily rebirth, renewal, fertility, and thanksgiving. The third tool was a stunning Sacred Self-offering Stick, whose use allowed him to continually offer his entire self for service to the Higher Powers. It is important to know that Fools Crow believed we can use these same tools to accomplish everything he did.

The Sun Dance is essentially a publicly performed ritual. It can be seen by anyone, and sometimes non-Indians are permitted to participate in it.[24] Therefore, what I have reported about it is not secret. Except for certain curings and healings, the Purifications Lodge is in the same category. Most of Fools Crow's thoughts and actions concerning it are presented in the first book, although the potent power that made the whole thing work for him was reserved for this second book. The Yuwipi ritual is a very private affair attended by people who are specifically invited. Sometimes this includes outsiders who are non-Indian. Fools Crow told me everything about his own participation in Yuwipi, and some of this information was reported in the first book. But out of respect for the medicine men who are still practicing this ancient rite on the reservations, I do not plan to reveal any more about it than I already have.

The Thought Transference Tool

In my book, *Secret Native American Pathways — a Guide to Inner Peace,* I tell about a visit I made to Fools Crow while he was guiding a vision quester at Bear Butte, and how he told me he had been sending his thoughts to and learning about the man, who was on top of the Butte while Fools Crow performed customary rituals at their Purifications Lodge in a meadow far below.[25] He had used thought transference to instruct the man to make four little crosses out of sticks, to place these upright in a row in front of him, and then to offer prayers to them. Making this kind of prayer item was an unheard-of thing to do, and certainly not a standard part of the questing procedure. Also, Fools Crow related to me the details of the vision the man had already received, and said further that I was to remain to hear what the man said when he came down from the mountain.

---

[24] For an account of the Sun Dance, there is nothing more complete than my own book, *Sundancing at Rosebud and Pine Ridge,* published by the Center for Western Studies, Augustan College, Sioux Falls, S.D., in 1978. Included in their research archives is my own movie film of the entire dance, and it is probably the only such in existence.

[25] *Secret Native American Pathways,* (Tulsa: Council Oak Books, 1988), pp. 215-216.

Then Fools Crow added that he would arrive within the next half hour. Minutes later, the man came walking down the winding trail, surprised and disconcerted to see me there with the holy man. When Fools Crow asked him to relate what he had seen, heard, and done during his four days and nights on the mountain, he squirmed even more, and I knew why. It was customary for only the quester's mentor to be told these personal things.

But the man obeyed, and what Fools Crow had revealed to me proved to be exactly what the man had experienced, including his being puzzled by a strange compulsion to make the four stick crosses. "Why did I do this?" he asked, after which Fools Crow looked at me and smiled broadly.

This was two-dimensional thought transference, and to say the least an impressive performance by the Old Lord of the Holy Men. That much I have already reported . . . but not the following:

When I first arrived at Fools Crow's camp, he was in the process of sending his thoughts to the man and also obtaining more information about the man's vision. It was now that I was shown the amazing secrets of how he did it. People commonly think that all thought transference and thought receipt is done by mental concentration alone. That was not so with Fools Crow. He had been given a better way by far — which explains why he could do it whenever he wanted to, and with a wonderful degree of accuracy.

He had seen me coming toward him across the lush meadow and stood up to greet me with a warm hug. As we exchanged greetings, I noticed that next to where he had been sitting on the grass was a cleared circular area about ten inches in diameter. The Cardinal Direction points were marked with little patches of colored cloth. In the center of the circle and standing upright in the ground was a stick that was perhaps a half-inch in diameter and eight inches long. It was wrapped in a piece of red felt that was held in place by a yarn belt that was done in the directional colors. Under the felt and next to the stick were a blue and a green feather — the colors of *Wakan-Tanka* and of Grandmother Earth. Although I could not see it, he told me that also under the felt was a lock of the man's hair and a little piece of his clothing. Tied to the belt with loops of yarn were a small stick-cross, a white breath feather, some beads, and a piece of sea shell. The stick itself was painted red, and had three black dots painted on it to make a face. "This is him," Fools Crow said as he pointed toward the unseen top of Bear Butte. "If I am sending thoughts to or getting information from a woman, the stick is painted Grandmother Earth's color, green."

Stuck upright in the ground at the west point of the circle's perimeter was another stick whose decorations were similar to those of the first stick. Fools Crow tapped it with his finger. "This is me," he said. He picked it up and turned it slowly as he showed it to me. "The things that are tied to this stick are personal things," he went on. "Here is a little piece of my ceremonial costume, and here is a piece of sweetgrass from my medicine bundle." He touched the piece of ceremonial costume and said, "I call my costume's shirt a 'war shirt,' but only because I wear it to war against things that are negative and not good. I did not fight in any wars with enemies or with any person, and I never wanted to. There is also a lock of my hair," he added, and then smiled as he rubbed the top of his grayed head. "The lock of hair is black. You can see that I put it in there many years ago."

As Fools Crow told me these things, I noticed there was an even more intriguing and beautifully decorated stick laying on a red cloth near the circle. It was much larger than the other two sticks. Fools Crow observed my interest in it and said, "That is my Self-offering Stick. I will tell you about it another time."

He needed no prompting to move on, and got down on his knees at the west point of the circle. He picked up a golden eagle tail-feather that was laying in front of him. "To transfer my thoughts to the other person, who is that stick in the middle of the circle, I first smoke the circle and myself with sweetgrass to purify us and get us ready. Beginning at the south where life and rebirth begin, I place the stick that is me at each of the Directions. Next, I close my eyes and relax myself by deep breathing. At each place as I move my stick clockwise around the circle I also close my eyes and concentrate upon the thoughts I want to send to the person. As I do this, I wave the feather toward him four times to push the thoughts in his direction.[26] When I am finished with the thoughts, the last thing I do is lay the feather down pointing toward the quester. Then I move my stick over the feather and up to him. When I get to where I am touching him, I make my 'whoo-whoo' sound to push my thoughts into him. He will hear me, and he will do what my thoughts tell him. At each of the directions, my thoughts are connected to the Person who lives there. I use the powers He sends me to shape the thoughts I am sending to a person. Sometimes, though, to have a little fun, I will tell the person to do some strange thing — like with the stick crosses. To do this, I must also tie something to represent what I want him to do to his stick. You see the little wooden cross there. The person always does what he is told, and then wonders why he did it. When he comes back from his quest, he will tell me about it and be very puzzled."

"Do you always use the two sticks for thought transference?" I asked.

"No. *Wakan-Tanka* can do it through me simply by my thinking about it, but using the sticks is the best and most effective way. As you see I am doing it today."

"And the sound . . . ?"

"Teach people to do this," he answered, "and they will be surprised at what happens. When they ask *Wakan-Tanka* to give them their own sound to use, He will do it."

"Did Stirrup teach you how to do this?"

"No, *Wakan-Tanka* and the Helpers gave it to me in a vision."

"I understand how you send thoughts," I said, "but how do you learn what the quester sees and is told in his vision?"

---

[26] Although I do not mention it every time he did it, Fools Crow always used four motions to make a ritual gesture. By this, he drew spiritual power into both the act and the ritual. For example, when he used his pipe and tobacco, he made four motions with the tobacco to the Four Directions, and then pressed the tobacco into the pipe bowl four times.

"I use these same sticks and circle, but I turn the feather toward myself when I am at each Direction. I also use my face mask. I put it on, and with my eyes open I begin at the south. I move my stick over the feather and up to the center of the circle where the quester is. When I get to him, I close my eyes and concentrate as hard as I can, asking the Person in that Direction to help me learn what is going on with that person. Then, still keeping my eyes closed, I look inside my forehead to see what appears on my mind-screen. I see pictures of what is happening, and I also hear words that are being spoken to the questing person. It is like being in a picture theater. The Person at the south will tell me how the things I am seeing and hearing are related to rebirth, renewed life, and destiny. At each of the Directions as I move clockwise around the circle I repeat this procedure, and I see on my screen additional parts of the picture. When I have been to all of the Directions and return to the south, the Persons assemble all of the parts on the screen, like putting together the pieces of a puzzle. The final pictures I see, together with the words I have heard, tell me everything of importance that the vision quester has seen and heard."

If the magnitude of his unearthly claims troubled him, Fools Crow gave no indication of it. Instead he fished around in his medicine bundle and came out with his face mask — a piece of red cloth that when unfolded was about eight inches square. It had two rectangular eye holes cut in it, and attached at the top corners were natural-colored string ties. White symbols had been painted on it in the distant past, but these were so faded they were barely distinguishable. My guess is that anyone finding this ordinary item in his medicine bundle would not have had the foggiest idea as to what it was used for.

At this point I exhaled markedly, and asked my standard question: "Can other people do this kind of thought transference, and for more than questing situations?"

He indicated that we can with a quick, "Ho," and gave his familiar affirming hand gesture. "If both people involved believe it can be done and call in the power, they can do it."

"Can it be done by people who are a long way apart, say one person in South Dakota and the other person in Los Angeles?"

He nodded and answered, "Even from England to South Dakota and back. Since I don't write letters, when I travel, I take my sticks with me, and I sometimes send messages home by thought transference." He started to chuckle then, and added, "No stamps and no telephone lines needed. Saves lots of money. Maybe we could sell this idea to the people, and all we would need then is someone to deliver packages!"

Dallas clapped his hands, and patted Fools Crow on the back. "You have a great idea, there," he said, "and maybe even better than Alexander Graham Bell, who invented the telephone. I'll buy some stock in your company."

"What advantage," I asked, "does using the sticks have over regular thought transference that is done only with the mind?"

"It is always the same where the concentration tools are concerned. Making them, purifying them with smoke, and setting them up and using them, all takes time, and during this time you sink deeper and deeper into communion with *Wakan-Tanka* and the Helpers. This gives Them the time they need to work in and through you, and they can accomplish more. It is the same thing as when we make our ceremonial costumes and paint our bodies. All of this takes time, but it is a way of going more intensely into the experience. We feel it more and we think about it more. By the time we do our ceremony, our daily life and any distractions have been put aside, and we are ready to receive the power and set it in motion. Naturally, the end result is far greater than it would be if we did not do these things."

"When you use the face mask," I asked, "do you lure with it?"

"Yes. I use the white cloud to pull the person to me."

"What do you do with the sticks after you have finished with them?"

"I tie the sticks as thank offerings to trees and bushes here on the sacred mountain. I keep the rest of the things to use next time. If we looked around here, and if the tourists haven't stolen them, we would find some of the sticks I have used other times."

"You did not mention a song in connection with this," I said.

Fools Crow rose slowly to his feet and stretched his arms and legs. Noticing that his small fire was close to going out, he walked over to it, stirred the coals with a stick and added a few branches. Sparks swarmed into the air like angry bees, and the rich fragrance of the sage-laden coals floated over to me. I closed my eyes and inhaled deeply. Bear Butte, with its purple-ash covered and rounded top, razor-sharp cliffs off to one side of the main butte, red mahogany, yellow pines, and thick grass, is a sublime place to be — an outdoor temple. To go there is to walk back into sacred Sioux and Cheyenne history — especially when you could be there with Fools Crow. This particular day, he had on his black cowboy hat, a small bolo tie with a turquoise stone in it, Levis, and a long-sleeved shirt with vertical white and yellow stripes. He adjusted the bolo so that it was centered on his chest and began to sing a Lakota song that had a pleasing melody. I caught only a few words that I recognized — something about how blessed we are to know *Wakan-Tanka*. When the song was finished, he studied me for a moment and said, "I am not given a song for everything, but there are always songs in my heart when I do these things because I am so happy."

Regarding transformation and thought transference, I describe in my earlier books numerous instances where the Higher Powers worked phenomenal things in and through Fools Crow. Among these instances were some where he was transformed, and some where — despite the unusual things that happened — he was not. Nevertheless, when a transformation experience ended, he could always turn some part of his dream or vision into tangible reality. If, for example, feathers appeared to him, he could snatch several of them out of the air and turn them into real feathers. On one occasion when I was with him, he did this very thing, and then handed the feathers to me.

To explain his ability to do this, he told me that what the white people often call "Indian origin myths" were actually stories that were built upon a foundation of historical truth, so that the stories are truth to the Indians, and are never referred to as myths. He believed that the use of the word "myth" implied that the stories were made up by human beings, and had taken shape over a long period of time — when, in fact, each one had begun as an ancient historical event. He knew that most of the stories were embellished and reshaped as they were told and retold over the centuries, but believed that the historical core always remained, and that people were not left on their own to develop their origin stories.

"There are," Fools Crow said, "legends our ancestors made up to help explain the existence and way of things . . . like those about the stars and the animal kingdom. But there is a big difference between legends and origin stories. The diggers (archaeologists and anthropologists) keep telling us how things were, but in my own lifetime they have made one discovery after another that has forced them to change their minds. If the diggers dig long enough," he went on, "one day they will find evidence that supports the historical truth of each of our origin stories. It is that way with transformation. There is always something real in it."

"How can people who are with you tell whether what you are doing is transferring thoughts or really happening?" I asked.

"When I am transformed and transferring thoughts, the person (or people — it could be to a group) will see what I am seeing, and also what is happening to me. Usually, even though I am wearing my regular clothing when we have gone out, after I have said my prayer my face will be painted and I will be in my ceremonial costume, which might also be painted. The message that comes to me when I am transformed will not be completely different from the messages I receive when I am not doing thought transference. What the white people call miracles happen in both instances. When the thought transference is finished, I will be back in my regular clothing again. But if what is happening is real, I will remain in my regular clothing, and I will not be painted."

I personally witnessed Fools Crow in both real and transference situations that were quite similar. I once saw a group of animals and birds come to speak to him while he was transformed into face paint and painted costume. Two other times though, I saw groups of animals and birds come to speak to him while he remained in his black hat and everyday clothing.[27] Once I saw him appear in ancient costume and face paint while smoke in the colors of the Directions swirled into and out of him, and dozens of immature golden eagle feathers glided about like drifting leaves in the smoke. That was the time he gave me the feathers.[28]

"What determines whether your situation will be real or one of thought transference?" I asked. "What is the point of having it happen both ways?"

He was surprised that I asked, and looked at me suspiciously. "*Wakan-Tanka* is only able to work with me in limited ways in a real

---

[27] *Fool's Crow*, 1979, pp. 183-184.
[28] *Secret Native American Pathways*, 1988, p. 7.

situation," he said softly. "I serve Him, but I remain a human being. My hands and arms and legs can only do so much. In thought transference though, there are no limits."

"Can you give me an example of a real situation that I can pass on to readers?"

"Yes, the curing of that man who had the tumor in his head, and *Wakan-Tanka* changed the mink skin I was wearing in my braid into a real mink who went to the man and sucked out the tumor. Twenty-three people, both whites and Indians, saw this happen. They were so surprised that they wondered if it really did. It did. There was no thought transference. No one saw me change into ancient costume or have my face painted. Then when the man went to the hospital the doctors could not find the tumor they had found earlier.[29] When animals and birds come to me, they either come in their earthly forms, in which case it is a real experience, or they come in their spiritual forms, where they can only be seen by anyone other than myself through thought transference. The difference in what this means is that the messages I receive from real creatures are limited to what has to do with things that are going on at earth level — at Kyle, Pine Ridge, Rosebud, or some other reservation. The spirit creatures bring me direct messages from *Wakan-Tanka*. They tell me what He is thinking about a certain situation and what He wants me to know . . . how to deal wisely with it and how to look into the future and predict things."

"And are both of these ways included in what can happen to other people?"

He raised his right hand in his usual affirmative gesture. "Hunh!" he grunted. "Anyone who is willing to lead the life I have led can do the things I do. I am out here on this remote reservation and am only here on earth for just a little while. Why would *Wakan-Tanka* limit these things to me? People all over the world have the same needs, and those who want to serve Him can be as big to Him as they want to be. The pity is that they doubt this and limit themselves. If most of the people in the world would accept this and live

---

[29] *Secret Native American Pathways*, 1988. pp. 219-220.

right, every physical and earth (environmental) illness would be gone in a little while, and it would be like living in the Garden of Eden again."

"How do you know about the Garden of Eden?" I asked.

"The Catholic priests told me," he said in an impish way.

Attempting to conceal my amusement, I asked, "Why are you smiling like that?"

"Because they only tell me the Bible stories," he replied. "They think I am not educated enough to understand more adult things. But in a way it is good. I tell the Bible stories to our people, who enjoy hearing them."

The Regeneration Tool

Early in the morning on another day, I went out to pray with Fools Crow. After numerous interruptions, we had been following a strenuous schedule to make up for lost time. Both of us were weary, and I expected that after prayer my eighty-six-year-old friend would want to return home and rest. But as was often the case, he surprised me — this time by engaging me in one of the most mesmerizing experiences of my life. We prayed for about a half-hour, and were both in the listening stage when he paused to open his medicine bundle and take from it two sticks — one that was made up to be himself after the same fashion as his thought transference stick, and another, slightly thicker stick that was probably eight inches long and sharpened on one end. To this latter stick were glued at their proper Cardinal Directions four small and rectangular pieces of colored cloth — white, black, red and yellow. Around the tops of these was wound a string of seven tobacco offering packets. Glued horizontally to the flat top of the stick was a tiny, carved, wooden buffalo with an erect penis.

Fools Crow used the pointed end of a small branch to inscribe on the ground a circle that was approximately sixteen inches in diameter. He then drew two lines that crossed in the middle to establish the Cardinal Directions, and placed a small piece of colored felt at each place where the lines intersected the outer edge of the circle — white for the south, black for the west, red for the north, and yellow for the east. Next, he stuck upright in the ground at the center of the circle the stick with the cloths and buffalo glued to it. This done, he reached into his medicine bundle and took out a small cloth pouch that was painted a dull red. He loosened the drawstring and poured its contents into his left hand. They were six small and smooth white stones, each of which had a circle painted on it in one of the Directional colors, plus one blue and one green.

"You already know what the colors mean," he said, "the Four Persons, plus blue for *Wakan-Tanka* and *Tunkashila*, and green for Grandmother Earth."

At this point he again reached into the medicine bundle and extracted from it a small straw basket, about the size of a bird's nest

and filled with a piece of red cloth. Next, he took out a piece of red string that was about twenty-four inches long. He tied one end of the string to the center stick, and the other end to the stick that was himself. The basket was placed next to the Tree, and he took his Self-offering Stick from the bundle, unwrapped it, and laid it on the red cloth alongside the Sun Dance circle. What Fools Crow had done was obvious . . . he had built a small replica of the Sun Dance circle, and he had tied himself to the Tree as the Sun Dance pledger does. He placed one stone next to each Directional color at the perimeter of the circle. The stone with the blue circle was placed above the north point, and the stone with the green circle was placed below the south point.

Fools Crow turned to me and said, "I will do the Sun Dance now."

As I speculated about what he intended to do, he quickly went into action. The day was already warm, and he removed his shirt (a male Sun Dancer does not wear one). He lit a braid of sweetgrass and used it to smoke the little circle, himself, and me. Then he knelt down at the south Direction, closed his eyes, and deep-breathed seven times to relax and to isolate himself from all other thoughts and distractions. He opened his eyes and picked up the white stone of the south. Holding it tightly in his closed right hand so that his attention was concentrated upon it, he sang four times:

> Person of the South
> Hear me.
> Talk to me about rebirth.
> Talk to me about new life.
> Talk to me about my destiny.
> Put the past behind me.
> Give me freedom from fear.

He put the white stone down, moved his stick up to the Tree and made his "whoo-whoo" sound, implanting the prayer he had just sung into the Tree. He took a few minutes to listen, then backed his stick away to the south point, after which he moved it clockwise to the west. He picked up the stone with the black circle on it, and this time his song was:

> Person of the West
> Hear me.
> Talk to me about purification.

Talk to me about renewal.
Talk to me about Thunder.
Put the past behind me.
Give me freedom from weariness.

He listened closely for a few minutes, duplicated his first actions with his stick, including his sound, put down the stone, and then moved clockwise around the perimeter to the north, where he picked up the stone with the red circle on it. Here his song was:

Person of the north
Hear me.
I am looking at the buffalo.
Talk to me about fertility.
Talk to me about health.
Talk to me about self control.
Enable me to create good things for all people.

He listened for awhile, then repeated the movement of the stick and made his sound. He returned the stick to the north, put down the stone, and moved to the east. He picked up the stone with the yellow circle and sang:

Person of the east
Hear me.
Talk to me about thanksgiving.
Talk to me about wisdom.
Talk to me about understanding.
I thank you for the past, the present, and the future.
I thank you for my friend, Tom, who is here to share this
with me.[30]

When he had done his listening, he put down the stone and moved his stick back to the south. *"Waste,"* he said, "good!"

---

[30] Fools Crow and Eagle Feather taught me that each day of the Sun Dance focuses upon a particular emphasis — the first day, rebirth; the second day, renewal; the third day, procreation; and the fourth day, thanksgiving. I have since learned that Joseph Epes Brown discovered something very close to this. At the previously mentioned Joint Symposium in Canada, Brown stated, "Concerning the Sun Dance there is one emphasis I would like to suggest here, and that is certainly the assertion that the renewal of world and life — re-creation — is essential. I would also like to emphasize, in the same context, that one should not forget this renewal also applies to man. That is to say, the man who undertakes the Sun Dance also goes through the process of interior regeneration, rebirth, renewal, and this is quite evident." *Native Religious Traditions*, Waugh and Prithipal, 1977, p. 148.

He untied the string at both ends, laid it on the ground, and picked up the little basket he had placed by the Tree. Then he said to me, "I will look into the basket to see what final messages the Persons have sent me. They always include some happy surprises." He pushed his finger into the cloth that was in the basket and probed around, exclaiming now and then in child-like delight with an "ah" or an "oh," seemingly oblivious to how it might look and sound to me as I watched a grown and brilliant man doing this. I did not, however, need explanations or convincing. I had already seen power come rolling out of one rite after another and become convinced that God worked in and through Fools Crow in prodigious ways.

As I have said, it is evident that what Fools Crow had done with this mental meditation tool was to do a miniature version of the Sun Dance performance, and in so doing he was able to experience in a short time all of the regenerating benefits of the great ceremony. Other men and women on the reservation were only doing the Sun Dance as an annual affair, but *Wakan-Tanka* had given the holy man a way to continuously experience the dance and harvest its powerful benefits. For Fools Crow, the dance had become an ongoing fountain of energy, transference, expansion, peace, fertility, and transcendence that he could call upon whenever he needed to.

"I was given this renewal tool during a vision quest at Bear Butte," Fools Crow said as he rose to his feet and bounced around, "and I have used it for nearly forty years. It has given me the vitality to keep doing the things the Higher Powers work in and through me. The work of a holy person can be hard. I am to use this tool for myself during my lifetime, but when I am gone you can pass it on to the world."

I had to admire his assurance that the world would be interested in all of this, but it came from *Wakan-Tanka*, and I was not about to argue with that. Fools Crow rumbled on. He was overflowing with energy, smiling, and ready to go. The regeneration had taken approximately an hour, and once we returned to his house we accomplished a great deal more with the book than we otherwise could have.

First, though, he turned to me and said, "Now you do it."

He had noticed my weariness just as I had observed his. Instead of waiting for a reply, he went to a nearby tree and snapped off a thin branch. Using his pocket knife, he paired this to a length of about six inches and brought it back. He sat down beside me and said, "Give me some things of yours to tie to the stick."

Not being prepared and not having with me anything that was small and could be easily attached to the stick, I wondered what I might use.

"Handkerchief and a key," he said as he held out his hand to receive them. He was beaming and felt very good. I could feel the energy and enthusiasm radiating out from him.

"What else?" I asked.

"Shoelace!"

I gave him one.

"Comb," he said and chuckled. He knew that, being bald, I probably didn't carry one, and he was right.

I shrugged my shoulders and held out empty hands.

"You have paper," he said after he had stopped laughing. "Write a prayer to the Higher Powers on a little piece and fold it up."

I did this, and handed the paper to him.

"That's enough," he said, and then rummaged around in his medicine bundle. He came out with a small piece of braided sweetgrass, a few turquoise-colored beads, a patch of red felt, two white breath-feathers, and some yarn. He deftly tied all of these to the stick, and added the items I had given him. "When you do this at home," he said, "add carefully chosen items to the stick — things that mean something important to you."

I did the renewal meditation then, following as closely as I could what he had done, except that my prayers were in English and not sung. Afterwards I felt absolutely superb and fully regenerated. It was as if the weight of the previous days had never existed. It had rolled away, and my creative thoughts were racing ahead.

"Whenever you have used any of the ritual tools you must afterwards deny yourself something worthwhile for a period of four days," the holy man said as he returned his paraphernalia to his medicine bundle and swept away with his hands all traces of what he had done on the ground. "This is how you tell the Higher Powers that you really appreciate what they have done for you. They will send extra blessings to you for this."

The Sacred Self-offering Stick

Two of the magical focusing tools have been described now, and only the third remains. While I haven't mentioned this item until this chapter, after Fools Crow let me see it the first time at Bear Butte, and also when he did his Sun Dance meditation, he didn't hide it any more, and I saw it a number of times as he did his private rituals. It was his Sacred Self-offering stick, a resplendent item that he kept in his medicine bundle in a special red cloth wrapping. He unwrapped it and laid it out alongside his other focusing tools while he did rituals, and he also put it down beside him when he went out to pray. He did not use it in the Purifications Lodge, or at a Sun Dance or Yuwipi. He did not, in fact, ever use it when someone else was sharing in a ritual — all of which leads me to believe that the stick must have been a very personal thing to be used when he was alone. Kate, and Fannie before her, were the only exceptions to this rule, and myself of course, so that I could see it and after his death pass along its description and the way he used it.

The first time he presented it to me, he held it with the greatest care, and I could see in his misting eyes and soft smile how much he cherished and respected it. If he did actually pass on his medicine bundle to anyone, I am certain that this beloved item was removed before the transfer was made, and then hidden away where no one could find it.

He handed me the stick and as I inspected it I could smell the smoked sweet-tobacco and sweetgrass that impregnated it. "I made this many years ago," he said, "in 1928, just after our two sons died. Fannie and I lost four out of five children to sudden sicknesses. I tried, but there was nothing I could do for any of them. But I wanted *Wakan-Tanka* and the Helpers to know that I did not blame them for the deaths, and that I would continue to serve Them. It is made up of things that represent me and my thoughts, along with my love and devotion to the Higher Powers. It also expresses my continuing gratitude for what the Higher Powers have done in and through me for others. I call it my 'Sacred Self-offering Stick,' and Stirrup, who had one of his own, taught me how to make and use it. He told me that in former times every medicine person had one. I was only a boy when he taught me, but he said I would know when the right time had come to make it."

In appearance alone the stick was a fabulous creation, and the thought of its not being with him in his grave troubles me greatly. Its base was a ten-inches-long and one-inch-in-diameter cottonwood stick. It was hand-carved and painted red. At its top end, which was rounded off slightly, he had painted on the front side three black dots to represent his own face. On the back side, extending from top to bottom, was a narrow, undulating black line. The stick was wrapped in a piece of red felt in such a way that the face was left exposed. Originally, he told me, he had used red cloth, but when that wore out he replaced it with the felt, which was quite new.

On the outside of the stick, about where belt level would be on a person, he had wrapped and tied four strings of thick yarn in the Four Directional colors — white, black, red and yellow. To this belt were tied two pouches, one containing tobacco and herbs, and the other sage and sweetgrass. Hung from the belt on string loops were two beautiful sea shells, some beads of different colors, and a white breath feather. Above the belt, a string of seven tobacco packets was wound around the stick.

Since it would have been difficult to do so, Fools Crow did not unwrap the belt and felt, but he told me what was underneath them. Tied upright to the stick were two long and dyed feathers — one blue and one red. The tips of these extended above the felt wrapping, and so could be seen. Also, there was a piece of the beaded turtle pouch that had once held a portion of his navel cord. There was a small fragment of cloth from the clothing of each of his deceased children, a scrap from the clothing of his surviving daughter, and a fragment from the clothing of each of his two wives. There was a bit of his first ceremonial costume — the one he was given when he was first made Ceremonial Chief of the Teton Sioux. The bits of clothing were kept in a small, woven pouch, together with four small rocks whose colors and shapes were different. Tucked under a string tie was some of the aging sage he had worn when he was Sun Dance Intercessor for the first time.

As previously indicated, the way all of this was assembled was simply stunning, and my illustrations will confirm this. The closest thing to it is the traditional Spirit Keeping Stick, which is illustrated in Chapter Fourteen. Fools Crow told me that he refurbished the Self-offering stick from time to time to keep it up to date and beautiful — so that it would please the Higher Powers. He added items that represented significant moments in his life, and he regularly replaced the tobacco offerings.

The stick was a very personal item, and I was not certain that he wanted to tell me anything more about it, but he did.

"I am fully wrapped up in this stick," he said as he caressed it lovingly. "It is my way of continually telling *Wakan-Tanka*, the Helpers, and Grandmother Earth, how much I appreciate the opportunity to serve them. Being one of their hollow bones means more to me than anything else in life. When I am busy with daily tasks, or when I need to go someplace, this stick continues to tell Them how I feel. Wherever I am, I know the stick is doing this for me, and that my thanksgiving is not being neglected. Because of this I love and respect the stick. Wherever I am, it is always in the back of my mind.[31] You must tell people to make their own Sacred Self-offering sticks and to put them out as I do. It will give them a feeling of closeness to *Wakan-Tanka* and the Helpers that nothing else can equal."

Impressed as I was, I had one more question. "What is the purpose of the undulating black line on the back of the stick?"

"My prayers fly up it on their way to the Higher Powers, and then their responses come flying back down it to me." Then he lifted up the felt wrapping where it covered the bottom of the line and added, "See, there is a little painted cup there to catch the blessings I know the Higher Powers will send me."

Cups! Positive thinking, I told myself. Fools Crow sits with cupped hands while he deep breathes to sink into full communion with *Wakan-Tanka* and the Helpers. The Apache Sunrise Ceremony girl sits with cupped hands on a sacred deer skin while she prays, knowing that for centuries on end God has not failed to fill the cups of her people and will not fail to fill hers!

---

[31] When Fools Crow said this, it made me think of the Pueblo Indians, who put prayer sticks, called "pahos," out in rock shrines, where Sun can pass over, see them, and pick up the spirit of the prayers to take them to the elders in the Underworld who "have the ear of Gna-tum-si," the Creator. The pahos continue to pray for them while they are occupied with daily tasks. To know this is happening is comforting, and it keeps them looking for God's answers, which they take for granted are on their way as soon as the prayer has been prayed into the paho and it has been placed in the shrine.

7 THE LIGHTS OF WISDOM

IN THE FOOLS CROW BOOK, I PRESENT MOST OF FRANK'S DE-
scription of what he did in the Purification Lodge, known to many
people as the "sweatlodge."[32] Included in this material is both text
and illustration describing how he cured when a patient was present,
and how he did this when the patient was absent. Given too is his
performance of an incredible ritual with stones that were placed cold
in the firepit, and which he caused to become red hot by spewing on
them a certain herb.[33]

What was deleted from these accounts is how Fools Crow was
able to do such amazing things as these, and why his accomplishments
in the Purification Lodge surpass those of most other medicine peo-

---

[32] Black Elk and Joseph Epes Brown also use the term "Purification Lodge," rather
than "Sweatlodge." The latter term has arisen more from its use for sweating out
bodily impurities, but the use of the lodge is far broader than that. Brown 1953, pp.
31-43.
[33] *Fools Crow*, 1979, p. 102.

ple. I only say "most" and hold out the possibility because I have no way of knowing what all medicine persons are accomplishing in their lodges. I would be delighted to learn that there are some out there who can equal, and even exceed, what *Wakan-Tanka* has done in and through Fools Crow. Nevertheless, I do know that Fools Crow was given insights regarding the Purification Lodge that in my personal experience have never been matched, and which contributed even more to the power that was stirred up and set into motion through him.

While we were talking about the Purification Lodge, I said to him, "Most Native Americans seem to think that the inside of the lodge dome represents either the womb of Grandmother Earth or the universe. Is that what you were taught?"

"That, and more," he responded as he raised his hands palms forward. "*Wakan-Tanka* taught me during one of my vision quests what the Purifications Lodge is. It is much more than a willow, half-dome-shape structure. Its true shape is that of a ball, and the bottom half of the ball is underground. Once the above-ground part is finished and covered over, and everything, like the sage and the other items I use, is in it, the Lodge becomes the dwelling place of *Wakan-Tanka* and *Tunkashila* above, of Grandmother Earth below, and of the Persons in the Four Directions. Then when I enter it and do my rituals I am sitting on the great plane of the earth in the midst of them all."

"It sounds," I said, "very much like your description of being surrounded by power."

"It is," he replied as he used a stick to draw a diagram on the ground to show me what he meant, "except there is a big difference. When I am surrounded by the Higher Powers, I call their powers in to me. But when I am enclosed with the Higher Powers, I can go to where they are and visit with them."

In case anyone is wondering, Fools Crow said this without the slightest indication of the magnitude of his claim. There was no shoulder or face language to suggest that I should doubt it. He just sat there and waited for me to go on.

"How do you go to visit them?" I asked.

"*Wakan-Tanka* has given me the power to travel in the spirit to where they are, and I go and talk with them."

"Do you do this while others are present in the Purifications Lodge?"

"No, except for Kate, who assists me by passing in the heated rocks from the outside fireplace, and then stays close by because she knows what is going to happen to me."

That last remark got my full attention, but I decided I would wait for him to explain it when he was ready. "How is what you do in spirit travel different than sending and receiving information through the smoke and the individual messengers who serve the Persons who are in each Direction?"

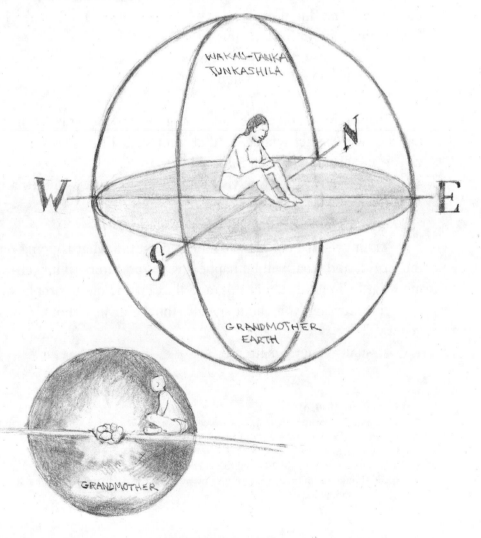

"It is a face-to-face thing. I see them."

"You see them?" I responded in surprise as I remembered the Biblical statement that no one could look upon God and live. "What do they look like?"

"Lights," he replied matter-of-factly, and waited for that to sink in.

"Lights," I murmured and leaned back in my chair. "Earlier, you told me that Joe Ashley told you what God looks like, and that you have lived comfortably with that idea. Is this what Joe said?"[34]

"Joe did not spirit travel," Fools Crow replied, "but what he told me was close to what I have seen."

"Are all of the lights the same color?"

"No. *Wakan-Tanka* is a huge white light. *Tunkashila* is a huge blue light. Grandmother Earth is a big green light. Each of the Persons is the color of his direction."[35]

I tried to absorb this while Fools Crow continued. "You want to know how I can visit with a light," he said.

"Yes."

"I speak to it, and a voice answers me out of the light. Each voice has its own distinct quality, so that I could, if I heard it someplace else, probably know who was speaking to me."[36]

"Did they, in your first visit with them, tell you who they are?"

"No. I knew from their colors."

"What kinds of things do you talk about?"

"Things that help me see and understand what is going on in the world, and what will be happening in the future. They also tell me what I should do about this, and they enable me to prophesy."

"Do they tell you about specific things, or just about things in general?"

"Usually general matters."

---

[34] *Fool's Crow*, 1979, p. 53.

[35] Brown points out that Black Elk associated *Wakan-Tanka* with Light, using a capital L. Brown, 1953, p. 42, and *Fools Crow*, p. 53.

[36] I find it pertinent that while Black Elk speaks of the six Powers of the world — the four Directions, plus the Sky and the Earth, he also speaks of Grandmother Earth as if she should be counted as a seventh Power. Neihardt, 1979, pp. 28, 166; and Brown, 1953, p. 32.

"Things that have to do with the entire world, or just about your Teton Sioux people?"

"Mostly about my people, but they give me some information about the rest of the world too."

"What do you talk about with Grandmother Earth?"

"Pollution problems and what we can do to save the earth."

"So, Grandmother Earth is concerned about her well-being also," I commented.

Fools Crow nodded gravely, and then continued, "She feels things just like we do, so to make her feel better another thing I do is thank her constantly for providing the food, the water, and the plants we need to survive."

"Is there more that you talk about with the other Lights?"

"My visions. They help me interpret them, and also the visions and dreams of people I am doing ceremonies with."

This prompted me to ask a side question. "Do you do visioning to interpret the visions of questers you are with at Bear Butte?"

"Yes, and also to interpret the dreams my people have in their regular lives."

"When exactly do you make these spirit trips? Is it every time you are alone in the Purifications Lodge?"

"Not every time, or even most of the time. The trips are special gifts, and usually happen during or just after some important event. I am in there and I get invitations from *Wakan-Tanka* and the Helpers . . . not all at once, but maybe one or two . . . whoever wants to talk to me. They are watching, and know when I need this."

"How do the invitations come?"

"Through the hot stones in the firepit. They speak to me and bring messages from the Higher Powers."

"And how do you travel from the Lodge to where they are?"

"I shake my rattle and sing my song. Then I lay my rattle down and pull my arms, bent at the elbows, tightly to my sides. With my eyes closed and my hands cupped, I concentrate as powerfully as I can upon the idea of my being lifted up. I begin to shiver, and I stomp my feet. Before long I feel myself preparing to soar up like an eagle into space. Maybe it is more like the first firing of a rocket as it begins to leave its launching pad. Pretty soon, I feel my body coming apart, and I both feel and see my spirit leaving it. My spirit looks like me, just like I look when I am in my body, and I am the same age. Up and up I go to where the Person is that I am going to visit. It only takes me seconds to get there, although I see myself speeding past birds, then clouds, then planets and stars. I even pass through what the white man calls the Milky Way."

"Then the Persons, even though they enclose you within the Lodge, are still a long ways away?"

"You must understand that while the Lodge is very little, only four feet high and eight feet across, when I am in it, it becomes as big as the universe itself. I do not feel confined, in fact I am not conscious of any walls at all. It is as if I am floating in space. This is a wonderful feeling, and I wish everyone in the world could share it. Then there wouldn't be any people who don't believe in *Wakan-Tanka!*"

"But the speed at which you travel . . . ?"

"I go faster than rockets do. I have heard about the speed of light, and what I do is more like that," he said and slapped his leg with enthusiasm. Then in a moment he grew quiet and his eyes softened. "Actually," he said, "this spirit travel I do has frightened both of my wives."

He knew that would get my attention, and waited for me to ask, "Why?"

"Because I faint when I spirit travel, and I remain unconscious until my spirit returns to my body. Sometimes I am gone for as much as two days.[37] Fannie and Kate have had to stay with me and watch over me during this time, and they have told me that sometimes they are afraid I have died."[38]

"Are you aware of time when you are out of your body?"

"No."

"Do you, as Black Elk did when he spirit-traveled, see your ancestors encamped in a beautiful land up in the sky?"

"No."

"Is anyone there with the Powers when you visit them?"

"No. All I see is the Lights."

---

[37] See *Black Elk Speaks,* for Black Elk's similar experiences with spirit travel and fainting, pp. 240-241.

[38] In telling about her dreaming, the Desert Cahuilla medicine woman Ruby Modesto reports that during dreaming the soul goes out of the body. On one occasion when this happened she was in a "sort of coma, asleep for several days." Her relatives were fearful for her, but had difficulty bringing her back. Once they did, they made her promise not to do it again until she knew how to get back on her own, which was to tell herself in advance that she was going to return. Modesto and Mount, 1980, p. 26.

"Do you credit the curings you do in the Purifications Lodge to your ability to spirit travel?"

"The stones in the firepit are given to me for this purpose. They get me all of the information I need about the person I am curing, and they also tell me what to do to help them."

"No one thing seems to be the answer for everything," I said.

"This is because *Wakan-Tanka* has been wise enough to make life challenging and interesting. What would it be like if there was only one way to do things? With *Wakan-Tanka*, life is a constant adventure where we are always finding new treasures. It never gets dull, and if it even starts to, He gives us new challenges and new ways to go. This is why people don't need drugs for excitement. With Him and the Helpers there is always more than enough."

"Is this why you use the Purifications Lodge for some curings, and other methods for others?"

"Yes, and *Wakan-Tanka* and the Helpers make these decisions for me. They know each patient's heart and mind, and which way will reach and work best for each. Medicine men and women do not need to worry about these choices, because they are usually given the power to cure only one thing. So they use the same ritual and medicine over and over again. This is true of Yuwipi men also. But *Wakan-Tanka* has used me to cure and to heal many things. You have seen this with your own eyes. The only things I still have trouble with are those cases that are too far advanced, or those I have never encountered before."

I understood what Fools Crow was saying. Research had shown me that in pre-white time the Native American medicine people had been able to cure in a remarkable way the illnesses and injuries they were accustomed to, and had had years to work with. But when diseases, such as smallpox, were brought in by Europeans and raged among the people, the curers were caught unprepared, and in desperation often resorted to treatments they had used for other illnesses that proved to be the worst possible things they could have done. One only needs to read the ghastly records of the swiftness with which these horrors struck the Indians to know that the medicine people had no time to seek out *Wakan-Tanka* and prepare. The diseases rolled through them like a rampaging flood, and took thousands upon thousands of Indian lives in the process. In a less abrupt way it was so with Fools Crow, and it was not until he was well along in years that he felt confident to undertake the treatment of ailments once unfamiliar to the Native Americans — like cancer, diabetes, heart disease, deformities, and mental illness.

"Spirit travel will be a mind-boggling thing for many of my readers," I commented. "Should I tell them that it is a thing they also can do?"

"Of course," he replied brightly, "but it will probably not happen until they have tried to do it several times. At least not until *Wakan-Tanka* and the Helpers know they are ready. As I said, this is a very special gift, and it is not given until it is deserved. It did not happen to me until I had become an experienced holy man."

As I turned to other things, I was still shaking my head in amazement. Spirit travel was a dreamland thing for me. "You have shown me how you can heat the stones in the Purifications Lodge without their being previously heated in the outside firepit," I said. "I know you were given a special herb to chew and spit on the rocks to cause this. Is there anything more that you do?"

He was holding up his hands again. "I sing a song that tells *Wakan-Tanka* I am ready for something to happen that no one else will believe. As I also told you, even my uncle Black Elk had to come and see with his own eyes while I heated the rocks before he would believe it."[39]

"What real purpose does this amazing gift serve beyond what you have already told me. You don't associate it with curing, do you?"

"It is living evidence of the way *Wakan-Tanka* blesses holy people who are willing to give their entire lives over to being His hollow bones. If the people who you tell this to are willing to live as I have, they will be given their own special thing — not the ability to heat the rocks perhaps, but something like it. The rocks and the medicine that heats them is something very special between *Wakan-Tanka* and me. That is why I have let only a few close friends, including you, see me do it."

---

[39] *Fool's Crow*, 1979 p. 102.

That was a surpassing privilege, and something I will never forget . . . the kind of thing no one will believe unless they see it with their own eyes . . . a true walking on water. My thoughts drifted back to that awesome night in the Purifications Lodge, and Fools Crow cleared his throat with a rumble to bring me back. I smiled and asked sheepishly, "Is there anything else that you do in the Purifications Lodge that you'd like to tell me about?"

He rubbed his chin and cheeks for a few moments, then his eyes opened wide and he made an exclamation motion with his right hand. "Uh," he grunted. "Sometimes *Wakan-Tanka* helps me take a good look at myself."

"How so?" I asked.

"He can read my heart and mind and soul, so He knows what is going on inside of me, but he also knows that I need to know what is going on too, so He has given me a way to learn this."

"Does self-examination require spirit travel or the talking stones?"

"No. He has given me a song to sing while I close my eyes and think about myself. When I have finished the song, I open my eyes and see an image of myself sitting on the other side of the lodge facing me. The only light is from the glowing rocks, so the image is bathed in a red glow and is shadowy. It just sits there and looks back at me. I stare at it and what I see tells me more than I sometimes want to know and admit. I see whether I am doing anything that might hinder the work of *Wakan-Tanka* and the Helpers, whether I am standing up for them, whether I am being a good reflection of them to others. You might think this is not necessary for me, but it is. I have my human weaknesses like everyone else. People who think they are beyond the need for this are mistaken, and one day — perhaps too late to do anything about it — they will be forced to face it."

"How are others to do this?" I asked. "Must they use a Purifications Lodge?"

"That is the best way, but I have been given a way to do it simply by drawing a line in front of me on the ground, and then putting (projecting) my image to the other side of it and facing me. This is something that should be done in soft light though, and by the red coals of a fire."

"The song," I said. "You have not sung it for me."

He looked away and his eyes grew moist as he started to sing.

> Great Ones
> Pity me.
> Help me look honestly at myself.
> Truth is coming.
> It hurts me.
> I am glad.
> You can make me better.

Dallas had been listening carefully. After he translated the song, he stood up and walked away to the edge of the Sun Dance circle which was west of Fools Crow's house. I joined him there.

"I am a devout Roman Catholic," he said with a sigh. "He does sacramental things, and he is also a Roman Catholic. But he did not learn these kinds of things in the church. He could though . . . we call it the Act of Contrition, and Penance follows it. But he doesn't confess or do penance. He doesn't agree with the idea and doesn't associate it with piercing in the Sun Dance. Piercing is thanksgiving, not penance. But he knows, he knows . . ."

All of the wonders had not yet been revealed. There was something else to come, and the walking on water continued.

On another day, Fools Crow sat with palms up and said, "I will tell you something no one else knows, not even Kate. Since to be a good and wise leader I need to learn exactly what is going on with my people, sometimes when I am alone in the Lodge — I never know in advance when this will happen and there is no warning — *Wakan-Tanka* transforms me into a bird or a dog or a cat, and then sends me out in this form to where I can fly over or walk about in Kyle or Pine Ridge or in some other place and see what people are doing and hear what they are saying. I can even go into their houses, and they will think I am just a stray animal. Later on, when I see them and tell them what they have been doing and saying they are astonished. When our AIM people were doing their brave holdout at Wounded Knee, I went in to talk with them thirteen times. But once when the situation was very tense because there had been shooting, the FBI wouldn't let me in. So I went to my Lodge, asked *Wakan-Tanka* to change me into a dog, and then went among the holdouts to see if they were all right. I have not told anyone else about this."[40]

"Is there any limit to how far you can go in these forms?"

"Yes. I only go to my own people." He chuckled then, and added, "I wish I could go into the White House and learn what the president is doing, or that I could sneak into the back rooms where congressmen or BIA people are planning things. Then I would know how to outsmart them and how to get our sacred Black Hills back!"

I shared his amusement, and then asked, "That day when we were together and you suddenly knew and told me something terrible had happened to some Indians in Pine Ridge (there was a shootout between Indians and FBI agents, in which two agents and an Indian youth were killed), you didn't go away then. How did you know?"

"I have done my traveling so often that I have developed the power to sense these kinds of things. This is another gift that will come to all people who serve *Wakan-Tanka*. And, I have something more than that — the stones in my left arm and hand, and the one on my back. They move around to tell me when something bad is going on, and they play a special role in my rituals in the Purifications Lodge (more information about these stones is given in Chapter 11, and in the Fools Crow book).[41]

---

[40] The ability of medicine people to be transformed into animals and birds and to travel about is frequently attested to in the literature of many tribes.
[41] *Fools Crow*, 1979, pp. 49-52.

8 WHITE CLOUDS

FOOLS CROW WAS TAUGHT THAT *WAKAN-TANKA* IS CONCERNED with human needs, and not luxuries. If we want luxuries, He has given us at birth the power to work for and obtain these. After the priests had talked to him about the Genesis stories, Fools Crow also understood that we are warned by the Tree of the Knowledge of Good and Evil that good is as threatening to us and our relationship with *Wakan-Tanka* as evil is. "When life is too good," Fools Crow said, "we think too highly of ourselves and our blessings. Then we decide we are the wisest and the favored ones, and we don't think we need *Wakan-Tanka* and the Helpers any more."

Upon hearing him say this, I remembered the dual role played by Pueblo clowns, and also by the Plains Indian "contraries" who always did things backward. The Pueblo clowns' responsibility is to cheer people up when they are downcast, but also to bring people "back to earth" when they begin to think too highly of themselves.

Within the contexts just mentioned, "luring" was among *Wakan-Tanka's* diverse gifts to the Native American people, and in the ancient days they practiced it regularly. Densmore relates how, on a wager, a Sioux medicine man put down a skeptical white doubter by luring a buffalo into sight and close enough for the white man to shoot it without his having to move from where he and the medicine man stood.[42]

As for the persistence with which luring has been done, Fools Crow learned that *Wakan-Tanka* and the Helpers wanted people to badger them for needs, not because these Higher Powers needed to know the hearts of the people, but because people themselves had to know the measure of their commitment to the task; did they want what they needed badly enough to put some real effort into obtaining it?[43]

Fools Crow lured in a traditional manner.

The ancient Cherokees fashioned luring masks to bring game closer and make it easier to kill. Each of the masks resembled in design the creature being sought. Some of the Plains Indians tribes had Women's Societies whose principal duty was to call the buffalo herds close, and their success in achieving this is attested to by the fact that the women continued to fill this role long after European intrusion. Even today, the Pueblo Indians use hunting fetishes to lure game. The Cherokees used face masks for luring. They didn't use hood masks because in luring they were inviting something in, and therefore they would not want to close it out as a hood mask would do. For luring, Fools Crow used a face mask, and he kept this in his medicine bundle so that it was readily available. I have already described this mask in Chapter Seven. Since one of its specific uses is for luring, however, I will repeat that the mask consisted of an eight-inch square piece of red cloth with tie strings attached. There was nothing on it to represent ears, and there were no holes for nose or mouth, but there were two rectangular eye holes cut in it.

"To use this mask," Fools Crow said with his hands palm up, "I first draw a (symbolic) picture on a piece of paper, or on the ground with a stick, to represent what I want to lure to me. Then I sit down facing it. I put on my luring mask, take my rattle in my right hand,

---

[42] Densmore, 1918, p. 210.

[43] Jesus tells a parable to illustrate this same point as he describes an old woman who pesters a judge until he gives in and does what she wants him to do.

and I close my eyes and breathe seven times to relax and to shut out distractions. I need to concentrate all of my thoughts on what I am luring. As I do this breathing I cup my left hand because I know *Wakan-Tanka* and the Helpers are going to fill me with answers to my prayer. Then I open my eyes, and as I focus on the picture I shake the rattle and sing my calling song. It goes like this:

"Ho, I am calling you.
Wakan-Tanka hears me.
You hear me.
Come to me.
You can not refuse.
Come to me.
I see you coming.

"I sing this song four times. Then as I continue to shake the rattle, I look off into the distance, out across a little clearing, and I see standing at the far side of it the thing I need. Whether it is a person or an object, it is just standing there and looking at me. I watch it for a minute or two, and then I close my eyes and look up at the inside of my forehead where my mind-screen is. Before long, a white cloud begins to form there. I tell the cloud to do its job, and the front part of it begins to move out in a tube shape toward the thing I need. It continues to stretch out until it reaches the thing I desire and encloses it. I put down the rattle. Then the cloud comes back to me bringing the desire with it. When it has come to me, I put my arms around the desire to possess it, and I thank *Wakan-Tanka* for it."

"Is that the end of it?"

"Oh no," he exclaimed. "It is never long before what I have lured to me really comes to pass. Maybe this is because *Wakan-Tanka* has helped me focus my mind on it, and so I am thinking and doing what I should to make it happen. But whatever it is, it never fails. Anyone can do this if it is being done for others, and the purpose is good. Sing my song — in this case people can use it exactly as I have given it to you. When I wanted Kate to be my wife, I lured her to me. She couldn't resist. Whenever there is something I don't have that I need to help someone else, I lure it to me." Then as he pointed a finger mischievously at me, he said, "You are married and don't need a girl, but if you did, you could use luring to get one."

"How about money?"

"You can lure what you need, but that fancy new car you drive, you had to get that with your natural power. Spiritual power is for other things."

"What if you need a beautiful costume to wear to ceremonies where you are making a special appearance?"

"Kate and I can make it."

This was certainly true. Kate had already made me a beautiful beaded belt and pair of moccasins. "Why is your luring mask red instead of white?" I asked, "since white would seem to go with the white cloud."

"My luring is always done for something for my people. Red is the color we use to represent our race, so I use that."

"Some television evangelists," I said, "claim that God blesses people who give generously to their cause. What do you think about this?"

"I have heard about that, and what they mean is, give generously to them," Fools Crow commented with a hint of sarcasm in his voice. "Lots of people have told me that with my curing powers I could become a very rich man by demanding high payments. But that is not what *Wakan-Tanka* wants me to do, and the power is His anyway. He has made it clear that being rich does not bring happiness, and that it takes people's minds away from Him. Sometime during their work [ministry] the evangelists will pay a big price for this misuse of power. No one abuses the things of *Wakan-Tanka* and gets away with it forever."

"Do you feel that *Wakan-Tanka* punishes people for bad behavior?"

"No. He doesn't need to. People take care of this on their own. I have been told that the Bible says we reap what we sow, and that is true."

"Can bad things be lured?"

"As I look at what is happening in the world and to my people, it seems that is so. Evil exists, and we see it in many forms. But we need to remember that Evil is only here with *Wakan-Tanka's* permission, and it is a constant reminder to us that we must stay close to *Wakan-Tanka* and the Helpers to survive. Of course, The Highest Powers know that our greatest happiness comes when we are close to Them."

When I repeated my question about bad things, he pressed his fist against his mouth and stared at the ground. Some time passed before he spoke. "People," he said as he chose his words carefully, "who don't know *Wakan-Tanka* and the Helpers can not lure good things from them. Evil knows this, and takes advantage of every opportunity they give it to tempt them. As we can see, people are easily captured."

"Why don't the Higher Powers interfere with this so that people won't be hurt?"

"We have every opportunity in life to have things different. Except for what happens in nature, we bring our own curses down on our own heads. My people blame the white man for all of their troubles. This is mostly true, but that does not excuse our willingness to accept it and even make it worse. We can quit the dole system and we can quit the drinking any time we want to. We can quit bickering and stand together any time we want to. Indians everywhere ruin everything by failing to stand together. They all want to be the chief, the one who runs everything. So we end up with nothing. While I do not agree with violence because it just makes more violence, the young men and women of AIM (The American Indian Movement), our college people, and the great ones like Matthew (Matthew King), Vine (Vine DeLoria, Jr.) and Tim (Tim Giago) have shown us how we can be a proud and independent people again. But too many of us here on the reservations have become weak and give up easily. They have even wanted to settle our claim against the United States Government for the return to us of the Black Hills for a few million dollars, knowing deep inside themselves that, once we did, the money would soon be gone and we would be worse off than ever. Instead, we should all be luring to ourselves good behavior and courage. We should all be turning fully to *Wakan-Tanka* and the Helpers, and one day everything would be much better for us. So many white clouds should be going out all over the reservations that from above it would look like the ground is covered with snow. *Wakan-Tanka* would look down and see this, and every need we have would soon be ours."

"Do you think this will happen?" I asked. "As we have talked over the past two years it seems that your opinion varies. Sometimes you hold out hope, and other times you suggest that there is no hope. What do you really think?"

Fools Crow sagged a little, and his countenance fell. He sighed several times, took a deep breath, and rubbed his gnarled hands together. "I try to stay cheerful," he said, "but *Wakan-Tanka* told me during a recent spirit visit that the wagon will have come for me and for many others of us before it will get better. If I have one remaining wish to be fulfilled it is that one day my people will stand up as one person and be counted; that they will call back their pride and say 'no more' to alcohol and to dependency upon the United States Government; that our traditional ways, the ways that made us great, will become the ways of all of our people again. I have tried many times to lure this, but I know now that all of the people together must lure it in order for it to happen."

It was a sad moment for the Old Lord of the Holy Men, and my heart went out to him. Plainly, this awesome tragedy, the relentless deterioration of his people and their living conditions for more than a century, would remain a sharp thorn in his heart until the wagon arrived at his door.

9 TALKING STONES

IT APPEARS THAT FRANCES DENSMORE DID NOT SEE THEM IN actual use, but she gives extensive coverage to sacred stones,[44] beginning with a quote from Chased-by-Bears as he explains their symbolism:

"The outline of the stone is round, having no end and no beginning; like the powers of the stone it is endless. The stone is perfect of its kind and is the work of nature, no artificial means being used in shaping it. Outwardly it is not beautiful, but its structure is solid, like a solid house in which one may safely dwell. It is not composed of many substances, but is of one substance, which is genuine and not an imitation of anything else."[45]

Densmore says that to acquire information, medicine men sent their stones long distances. After a time the stones returned and gave them the desired information. The owner was the only one who could understand what they said, and therefore he was the only one who

---

[44] Densmore, 1918, pp. 204-251.
[45] Densmore, 1918, p. 205.

could tell others what this was. "During a demonstration for the curing of the sick it is said that the stones, flying through the air in the darkened tipi, sometimes strike those who have refused to believe in them." In referring to this movement of the stones, Densmore's informants expressed the opinion that sacred stones were representatives of "that which stirs," a Helper too subtle in essence to be perceived by the human senses. His symbol is the stone. He lives in what is termed "the four winds," and "it is he who sends the winds when they are called in." Here we have distinct evidence of an ancient view of power in motion in terms of having to be "stirred" to achieve a goal.

In former days, men who dreamed of stones were considered to be especially blessed. Typical of these as reported by Densmore was Brave Buffalo, who was born around 1838, was a prominent medicine man of the Standing Rock Reservation, and was the son of a leading medicine man of the tribe. Brave Buffalo states that:

> When I was 10 years of age I looked at the land and the rivers, the sky above, and the animals around me and could not fail to realize that they were made by some great power. I was so anxious to understand this power that I questioned the trees and the bushes. It seemed as though the flowers were staring at me, and I wanted to ask them "Who made you?" I looked at the moss-covered stones, some of them seemed to have the features of a man, but they could not answer me. Then I had a dream, and in my dream one of these small round stones appeared to me and told me that the maker of all was *Wakan-Tanka*, and that in order to honor him I must honor his works in nature. The stone said that by my search I had shown myself worthy of supernatural help. It said that if I were curing a sick person I might ask its assistance, said that all the forces of nature would help me work a cure.

Soon after this dream Brave Buffalo found on the top of a high butte his first sacred stone, which was still in his possession in 1911. He cured many illnesses by means of a spherical stone, which he said was a brother of the first stone he found on the top of a high butte. He explained that such stones are not found buried in the earth, but lay in the open on top of high buttes. They are round like the sun and moon, and obtain their shape by watching them — so they are related to one another. The Thunderbird was also said to be related to these stones. A medicine man was allowed to sell some of the round stones he found — the "helpers," who were considered to be brothers of his sacred stones — but he must not part with "the stone which was the center of his power."

Each medicine man composed at least one song to use with his stones during curings. This song was to be sung when any request was made of the stones. Densmore records a number of fascinating accounts of things done by medicine men who were the possessors of stones. In one, the stone brings a buffalo so close it can be killed. In another, lost property is found. One predicts precisely what will happen to a party on a war expedition. When asked to inquire of the sacred stones to secure information regarding the Crow Indians, Shell Necklace prepared a place on the ground and covered it with a red blanket. The stone was sent off and when it returned Shell Necklace covered himself with a buffalo robe, head and all, and asked what news it brought, which turned out to be exactly what occurred. Two of the accounts describe Yuwipi-like situations in which the medicine men were tied up — like Bear Necklace, whose arms were tied behind him, and then his fingers and toes were interlaced with twisted sinew. He was then wrapped in a buffalo robe and tied with ropes. His medicine drum, medicine bag, and a bell were hung high on the tipi poles, and he was laid on the ground beneath them. The tipi was darkened, he sang a song and told his dreams. Then the tipi began to tremble, the articles hanging from the pole dropped to the ground, his cords loosened, and he stood entirely free. There appeared before him a row of four or five small round stones ready to tell him what he wanted to know. Sitting Bull was present and made an offering of a buffalo robe to the sacred stones and asked that he might become famous (this request was certainly granted, for no one has ever become more famous than he). Bear Necklace wrapped one of the stones in buckskin and gave it to him. Sitting Bull wore it in a bag around his neck to the time of his death, and it was buried with him. Bear Necklace then gave correct information concerning an absent war party . . . and afterwards the stones always told him the names of those who were killed in war, the names of the survivors, and the day on which they would return. This information was always correct.[46]

Densmore reports that treatment of the sick by means of the sacred stones and by conjuring had been forbidden by the Government in recent years (sometime before the turn of the century), but that certain of the old men were allowed to continue treating the sick by administering herbs.[47]

I was, of course, delighted to learn that Fools Crow had been led to carry on this wonderful heritage, and in the first part of his story, he talked at length with me about his own sacred stones and the roles they played in his life as a holy man. He had in his possession three small sandstones — two that were round like a ball, one of which had a red circle painted on it, and one that was shaped like an egg — that he carried in his medicine bundle and used for certain healings. He had seven stones that were implanted in his body during an encounter with *Wakan-Tanka* at Bear Butte in 1965.[48] The stones used in the Purifications Lodge firepit spoke to him at certain points during a ritual.[49] And he had 405 White Stone Men Helpers that were given to him in his initial vision quest.[50]

Since there were so many different stones, I asked Fools Crow whether there was a single message that all of the stones together brought him.

"The stones stand for eternity and eternal truth," he replied. "We also realize that when a stone speaks, we are being told at the same time that with *Wakan-Tanka* and the Helpers, everything is possible. If a stone person can speak, it is proof that there is life in all things."

"The sandstones in your medicine bundle, how do you use them?"

---

[46] Densmore, 1918, pp. 217-218.
[47] Densmore, 1918, p. 245.
[48] *Fools Crow,* 1979, pp. 181-184.
[49] *Fools Crow,* 1979, p. 101.
[50] *Fools Crow,* 1979, pp. 50-51.

"*Wakan-Tanka* uses all of my stones as hollow bones to talk to me, to work through me to cure illness, to predict what will happen in the future, and to locate lost people or objects."

"Do the stones have their own spiritual power . . . are they able to do these things in and of themselves? Could you, for example, place a sacred stone on someone and it would cure them, and could they place one on themselves to accomplish the same thing?"

"I have told you that each created thing is given natural power. Stones also have spiritual power. But this spiritual power must be stirred up by ritual use, so the stones work together with individuals like myself who are also hollow bones. It is a very ancient way. Usually, a medicine person holds the stone in their hand or lays it on a patient and it talks to the medicine person. Sometimes I tell the patient to hold the stone in their mouth. I can also talk with heated stones that are in the lodge firepit."

"Then the stone can't actually cure, but it tells you how to do the curing?"

"The first thing it does is to determine the cause and the location and nature of the illness or other problem. Sometimes, the spirit of the stone steps out of its body and goes inside the person to look around until it finds the illness and its cause. The stones also have other ways to tell where illnesses and causes are. When it finds these, it comes back into its body and tells me what it has discovered. Then it takes me to where the right herbs or roots will be found to cure that illness or problem. Finally, it tells me what kind of curing method to use."

"How does the stone take you to a medicine plant?" I asked.

"Easy," he said with an air of assurance. "I hold the stone in my right hand while I cup my left hand. Then I walk around either in the area where I live, or where I feel led to go. As I walk around, the stone pulls my hand in the direction it wants me to head, and I follow. The pull is strong, and I have no choice. When we arrive at the place where the right plant is, the stone pulls my hand down to the plant, which may be a kind of medicine I have used before. Of course, I am not always led to curing plants by the stones. Sometimes, the Higher Powers just lead my mind, and I follow it to where the plant is. As soon as we arrive there, I know which is the right one.

Later on, I was able to witness Fools Crow's use of a stone (the one with the circle painted on it) in the treatment of a patient whose face was beet red and who had great difficulty breathing. He had the man take his shirt off and lie face down on a Pendleton blanket. Fools Crow marked the corners of the blanket with pieces of cloth that were the colors of the Directions, and then placed sage on the blanket. Then he chanted a "finding "song four times while he rolled the stone over the man's entire upper torso as the man turned from side to side and finally over on his back. This rolling of a stone was a technique Densmore reports was used by Brave Buffalo to locate an ailment.[51]

Fools Crow sang:

> Ho,
> We are looking for you.
> You can't hide.
> This stone is coming in there.
> It is *Wakan-Tanka's* eyes.
> It will find the sickness.
> It will find the cause.
> Then it will tell me.
> Soon you will be gone.

As I listened and watched with fascination, the stone reached the left side of the man's chest and a spot just to the right of the nipple. It stopped rolling, and Fools Crow couldn't budge it.

"The illness is under here," Fools Crow said to the patient. He pressed gently down on the stone and the man gasped from the pain. "You have a lung problem," Fools Crow continued, "your lung is poisoned."

Then the holy man held the stone in his right hand and with his left hand pulled a blanket over himself until he was entirely covered with it. He chanted, and afterward was quiet for a period of at least ten minutes. Then he removed the blanket and turned to the patient, saying, "The stone and my mind-screen agree. They both say you have poisoned water in your left lung."

While the patient watched apprehensively, Fools Crow took from his medicine bag a hollow bone-tube that was about three-quarters

---

[51] Densmore, 1918, p. 246.

of an inch in diameter and seven inches long. It had sinew wrappings on both ends, but was otherwise plain. He pulled a medium-sized enameled bowl up close to him, took one end of the tube in his mouth, put the other end of it on the man's chest, and began to suck on it. I could hear a distinct gurgling sound. Shortly thereafter he closed off the bottom end of the tube with his forefinger, and poured the tube's contents into the bowl. Enough greenish liquid to fill the tube came out. Fools Crow repeated this procedure at two-hour intervals, four times each day for four days, and each time the tube was filled with liquid that became subsequently clearer with each treatment. By the final, or sixteenth time, the bowl was filled, but there was no liquid coming into the bone-tube; it was empty. The man was experiencing no pain, seemed much better, and went happily home.

When the opportunity came, I asked Fools Crow to tell me how the curing stones talked to him. "You will only tell this after I am gone," he said, and reached into his medicine bundle to get one of the stones to demonstrate with. "You have noticed," he went on, "that when the stones talk to me I am in the dark with them. Once we are covered, I sing a 'thank you' song to the stone, telling it how much I appreciate the fact that it wants to help me. I sing this song four times, and then I wait, holding the stone like this, in the open palm of my right hand. In a little while, the stone starts to turn red and gets very warm. Sometimes it nearly burns my hand, and I'm sure it would seriously burn the hand of someone who did not know how to hold it. Then the stone begins to make a crackling and popping sound, which turns into Lakota, and it speaks to me, giving me information about the patient and what to do to cure them. When I know everything I need to know, the stone turns cold, and we are finished. Then I use the treatment the stone has told me to use."

"Is this always the way the stone works?"

"Pretty much," he answered as he put the stone back in the bundle, "although two curings are never exactly the same. The same basic steps are followed, but something special is done for each person because each person is special to *Wakan-Tanka* and has special needs. I will tell you now how my stone thank you song goes, but I will change it just a little so that no one will ever learn my exact song. As I have told you, each person who wants to do what I do must ask *Wakan-Tanka* to give them their own songs."

> I behold now this stone.
> It has power.
> I see it. I feel it.
> This power comes,
> And I can use it.
> I am thankful for it.
> I will help it work.

"What," I asked, "did the stone tell you about the cause of the poisoned lung?"

"It said he smoked too much, and that there was something in the tar."

"Tar," I remarked, "what would tar have to do with out here on the reservation?"

"He works on the highway crew that repairs our roads."

"Then there is a chemical problem," I said.

"This is what the stone told me."

"Have other patients come to you where these same causes were pointed out?"

"Yes."

In the first book, Fools Crow explains about the seven stones in his body that appeared suddenly while he was inside the cliff at Bear Butte in 1965, where either *Wakan-Tanka* or Grandfather *(Tunkashila)* spoke to him.[52] One stone was in his back, just below the left shoulder blade, and the rest were just under the skin of his left arm and hand.[53] On one occasion he had me feel the stones and move them around to show me how easily it could be done. It was uncanny, since they could be moved an inch or more in any direction — although each time I moved one, he had me move it back to its original position. The stones ranged in size from one-eighth of an inch to one-quarter of an inch. They were round, smooth, and hard as any rock is.

---

[52] I want to note here that while Fools Crow called this event a vision, he made it clear that it was something that literally happened to him. *Fools Crow*, 1979, p. 181.

[53] *Fools Crow*, 1979, p. 183.

He told me how the stones knew when a bad incident was about to take place. They began to move rapidly around. Then he would pray that people's hearts would change and the bad would go away so that good could replace it. Also, when he prayed each day the stones gave him messages from *Wakan-Tanka* and the other powers.

What Fools Crow added during a hands-up period, and I can report now, is that when he was in the Purifications Lodge, at one point in the ritual all of these stones began to move rapidly around under his skin. Whenever they passed close to one another, they would give off showers of sparks — about like what happens when someone throws a new log onto a smoldering fire.

"Many people," he said, "have seen these sparks and wondered how I made them. I only told a few of them how it happened. Some medicine men have secretly thrown dried pine needles onto the hot rocks to make sparks. If they practice this they can easily do it in the darkened Lodge without anyone noticing. Others have learned to make rattles with holes in the shell and have pieces of flint inside that make sparks when the rattles are shaken. They never tell people how they do this. They just let them think that it is the spirits' work. My sparks are truly *Wakan-Tanka's* doing, and He has a reason for this."

I could appreciate what Fools Crow was referring to, for I had seen both kinds of sparks made in Purifications Lodges. But these made only scattered and sporadic sparks; Fools Crow's showers were so thick they formed columns that ascended to the highest point of the Lodge.

"What is the 'reason' you referred to? What do the sparks indicate?"

"You know that fire is a piece of Sun on earth," he answered, "and that the warmth of Sun is really the warmth of *Wakan-Tanka's* person. When the stones are sparking, *Wakan-Tanka* himself has entered them and their activity is his moving swiftly around to let me know He is in there. If a person touched the stones in my body during this time they would burn his hand."

"Don't they burn your arm and back?"

"No. I feel warmth, but that is all."

"Why does *Wakan-Tanka* come in these instances?"

"This only happens when the illness that is being treated through me is a very serious one. *Wakan-Tanka* is like the good teacher; after his pupil is taught, He usually stands back to see what the pupil can do. But now the situation is too grave for that, so He comes to take over."

"Doesn't He — in the sense of your being a hollow bone — always take over?"

"Not like this. Together with concentration tools, he usually makes use of the natural and spiritual talents that have accumulated and developed in me over the years. He honors me by allowing me to contribute to the curing."

"Once He takes over, what does He do?"

"There is a mood in the Lodge that is unlike any other time. It feels like it is filled with pressure and energy. My body tingles and shakes from it. This happens to the patients too. They don't know exactly what is going on, but they know it is something awesome, mysterious, and even frightening. Loud sounds are heard of eagles and hawks crying and animals roaring, along with claps of thunder. We will hear singers singing, and drums and rattles playing. Usually, the Lodge itself begins to shake and rattle. The offerings that are tied to the roof swing back and forth. Sometimes, a steaming rock will even jump out of the firepit. Often, the people will cry out that they feel something very hot, like a large hand, touching their bodies. Then they will say they feel this hand pulling their illness out of them, and that it really hurts. By the time the ceremony is over, and it sometimes goes on for an hour or more, these people are always completely cured."

"No matter how serious their illnesses?"

"Yes."

"Then why don't you take all of your patients into the Lodge?"

"I told you that *Wakan-Tanka* makes the decision for me. He has His reasons, and I do not ask what they are."

"Apparently," I said, "the former medicine people did not know about this personal coming of *Wakan-Tanka* to the Purifications Lodge when smallpox and other plagues came. How would you explain this?"

"I do not know about any other holy person who was given this special power, and I do not know anyone who has stones in their body. But other holy men have received some powers that I do not have. *Wakan-Tanka* works with each hollow bone as He sees fit."

"How did you learn all these things about the stones in your body?"

"The Person who spoke to me in the cliff at Bear Butte told me everything, and ever since then it has happened just the way He said it would."

"Did you see a Light while you were in the cliff?"

"Yes."

"What color was it?"

"White."

"Then it was *Wakan-Tanka* himself who spoke to you?"

"I think it was, but that was a tremendous experience, and I was so overwhelmed by it that I did not see or hear everything distinctly."

On another day we continued to talk about stones. "So," I said to begin the conversation, "you have three healing stones, plus seven talking stones in your body. You've also mentioned the stones that are used with the Sun Dance tool, the stones in the Purifications Lodge firepit that talk with you to give you messages from *Wakan-Tanka* and the Helpers, and you have 405 White Stone Men Helpers.[54] Obviously, stones play a role of major importance in your life as a holy man. Is there anything about the White Stone Men that you haven't told me, but that people ought to know?"

His mind still sharp, the old holy man quickly replied, "I have not told you why in most instances only some of the White Stone Men come to help me with a curing or healing." He took a stick and drew a large circle on the ground. "This is the whole world," he said as he used the stick to point at the circle. "The 405 White Stone Men help people everywhere who love *Wakan-Tanka*, not just the Native

---

[54] An extended description of the White Stone Men helpers is given in my *Fools Crow* book, pp. 49-52, 81, 88, 93-94, 121, and 186. The Stone Men are divided into four groups, each of which has specific powers.

Americans. Some of the White Stone Men are busy here, and others there . . . in China, or Africa, or Germany."

This made me think of my friend, Zubi Credo, head chief of the Zulu medicine people in South Africa, who told me that he has a great number of spirits who come to help him when he cures and heals. I told Fools Crow about him, and what I said about the numerous spirits pleased him immensely. Then I added, "And you have said that different stones are equipped to help with different things."

Fools Crow confirmed this with a clenched fist and a quick, "Ho!"

"Why is it," I asked, "that it is your patient who is told the number that will come to the Purifications Lodge for a curing, and then makes a string of tobacco offerings in that number to let you know how many there will be? Why aren't you the one who is told this?"

"Because *Wakan-Tanka* wants to begin to build up the patient's faith even before he comes to the Lodge to be treated. The Higher Powers want to get the patient involved in every way they can, to get their mind centered on curing, and by doing this they increase the confidence and assurance of the patient."

"Sometimes," I interjected, "all of the 405 White Stone Men, who you also call 'Good Spirits,' come to the Purifications Lodge and to your Yuwipi or Sun Dance. Aren't some of them busy elsewhere?"

"You will notice that I say they all come, but I do not say they all stay. They all come to make a quick visit to let me know they support me, but then most of them return to what they were doing."

"If," I persisted, "the stones come to be with you, even briefly, then they will have left their patients. Isn't that a problem for the sick person?"

"The Higher Powers," Fools Crow replied patiently, "are not governed by time as we are. They can be gone, but will still not be gone, because there is no clock where they live. Everything they do is done at once. I could make a true puzzle by saying that they are back at the same time as they left."

"How can you be sure they are all present for what to us, with our clocks, seems like a moment?"

"Because I have been told that as many will come as there are tobacco offerings. If I or the patient make 405, that many will come.

And if someone is trying to trick me, such as George Iron Cloud did at that Yuwipi I told you about, all 405 White Stone Men will come and stay until they have taught him a lesson. You remember that George tried to hold on to the tobacco string while I was tied up and the lights were out, so that no one could steal the string by some trickery. He thought he had it, but when the lights were turned on, the string was gone, and he was flabbergasted. He was holding on to nothing but his imagination. The 405 White Stone Men did that to him, and he never tried it again."[55]

"The White Stone Men appear to be a gift to Native American medicine people, and to medicine people around the world," I said. "Would the Stone Men also be available to non-Indians who would like their help?"

Fools Crow gave a quick nod. "Since the White Stone Men are already helping out around the entire world, they will also be there for those who entrust themselves to *Wakan-Tanka*, and then use tobacco offerings to call them in."

---

[55] The full story of George Iron Cloud and the Yuwipi is told in *Fools Crow*, pp. 185-187.

10 HOW BIG?

WHEN FOOLS CROW SAID TO ME, "NOT EVERYONE CAN BE CURED, but everyone can be healed," I knew what he meant, for I had heard this from the medicine men of several tribes. As with other things that he said, however, I wanted him to verify that he meant the same thing.

"Why," I asked, "do you make the distinction between curing and healing? How do they differ?"

"Curing," he answered, "is spiritual, but not in the same way as healing is spiritual. People do die. Not everyone is cured. I have not asked *Wakan-Tanka* why this is so. I also know that He does not take a person out of this world. That would make Him responsible for all deaths, including the tragic ones. If it seems to Him that a person can not, or should not, be cured, for whatever His reasons, He may decide to not interfere and change the situation. He just lets them come to Him. On the other hand there are those times when He does decide to interfere and keep the patient alive. Death, though, is not a bad thing, since after it we go to be with *Wakan-Tanka* forever. In fact, this is what we are born for . . . born to die, for death is really the beginning of the great life that He has in store for us."

"You have already told me," I said, "that in your visions you learned that after death every person goes into one of three spirits, and remains in these until judgment day, when *Wakan-Tanka* will separate the spiritual people from the unspiritual. Spiritual people will go to a happy place, and the rest to a path where they will suffer all of the time.[56] What do you mean by suffering; what have you been shown about this?"

Fools Crow's lips tightened, and they hardly moved as he replied. "I said that people make their own punishments here on earth. That might be enough to satisfy *Wakan-Tanka*. But I would not blame Him if he really does shut the door. The way they think, and the way they turn their back on Him deserves this."

"What," I asked, "does a shut door mean?"

"That the dead person's spirit will drift around forever with no place to land. Now and then it will pass by the happy people who are with *Wakan-Tanka*, and will see what it has missed."

"This sounds a little like the Roman Catholic idea about Purgatory," I commented, wondering if that was where he got it.

"This idea is older than the coming of the black robes," he replied, "but I still hope that the spirits will not be required to drift forever. Anyway, since there are no clocks there, it will be different for them than it is here on earth."

"And healing?" I asked. "What about healing?"

"Healing is purely spiritual and has to do with helping a person to be right with *Wakan-Tanka*. Then if death does come, the person can die peacefully and not be angry or resentful about it. He learns through the healing rituals to think in terms of the quality of life rather than the quantity of life. Healing is a priceless gift that can be given to anyone who will accept it."

"It still seems," I responded, "like *Wakan-Tanka* is making a choice where the life or death of a person is concerned."

"*Wakan-Tanka* and *Tunkashila*," he replied firmly, "are more concerned about the survival of the nation than they are about the survival of any one individual. That is why, in the Sun Dances, we

---

[56] The full account of this view of life after death is given in *Fools Crow*, p. 47.

make both curing and healing available to everyone who wishes to receive them. The dancers become hollow bones during the four days of dancing, and they lay their hands on people to pass on the power for curing and healing that has filled them as they've danced their prayers. They spread strength and hope so that our nation will be uplifted and will want to continue on into the future. One person can not assure this, but a healed and united nation can."[57]

"How important is faith to the curing process?"

"It won't happen for us in its greatest way without faith."

"But unbelieving people are cured every day," I said.

"The body is an amazing thing," Fools Crow replied with a touch of steel in his voice. "*Wakan-Tanka* has made it in such a way that most illnesses will cure themselves without a medicine person's help. If people just waited awhile, their illnesses would go away on their own. But they become impatient and frightened, and know that a medicine person or a white doctor can speed up the curing by giving them something that will start the body doing what it is capable of."

"Have you been taught that the mind is responsible for many of our illnesses?"

"I know that the way a person thinks can make the body sick, and it can make the body well. But this does not include every kind of illness . . . for example, the contagious ones, or broken bones or injuries such as very serious burns. They will come in spite of what we think. White people who have visited me have said that we can avoid colds and pneumonia by just thinking them away. That might work sometimes because the thinking will cause those who believe this to live more carefully, but sooner or later, they will get a cold. Many of us out here on the reservation have died of pneumonia. I

---

[57] For comparison, in traditional Apache curing rituals the healing efforts intensify when it is determined that the patient is terminal. Anyone who is mystified by this needs to remember that, as Fools Crow has said, healing is essentially done for the sake of the community. What happens is that attention switches to the mourners, who will need added strength and comfort after their friend and loved one is gone. The Apache begin to lay hands upon and to pray for one another, so that the blessings spread. So long as the patient remains conscious, he sees this, and passes on with this final memory. It is a wise and good thing, and something we in the outside world would benefit from, were we to emulate it.

lost my children to this." He stopped to brush a fly away from his face, thought for a few moments, and then continued. "Balance is also important where illness is concerned. If we keep everything in balance we are in harmony with ourselves and are at peace. Maybe balance is the best illness fighter in the world."

"Even better than you?" I asked with a smile.

"Even better than me," he said and smiled back.

"Better than *Wakan-Tanka* and the Helpers?"

"No. I said in the world. They surround the world." He was pleased that he had escaped my trap and was smiling again.

"When patients come to you bringing tobacco to smoke and ask you to cure them," I said, "I know that you look into their eyes to learn whether or not they truly believe in your ability and desire to cure them. I know also that you learn by this whether or not they have faith in their own ability to contribute to the healing, and above all whether they have faith in *Wakan-Tanka's* promise that He will send the power for this. Is looking into their eyes all you do?"

Fools Crow grew as resolute as ever I saw him. His chin lowered, his shoulders moved back, and his chest protruded. "The first question is always, how big is the person's faith? Without a big faith," he continued, "there is nothing I or *Wakan-Tanka* can do to cure or heal them. Faith is the first thing that brings the spiritual power in. Of course, the rituals and the tools play a part in this, but without faith there is no power and there is no movement."

"But do you do more than look into their eyes?" I persisted. "I've noticed that while you do it you sometimes place your right hand on their shoulder."

He smiled broadly. "You believe to see," he said. "You are one of us!"

I felt a tightening in my throat, and held back tears. It was a great compliment from the Old Lord of the Holy Men. His hands went up, and I got ready with my notebook.

"As we continue together," he went on, "you will notice that I always place my hand on the people's shoulders. You just didn't see it at first. I do touch them with my eyes, and I do see them with my mind, but I also lay my hand on their shoulders — and this is what tells me the most. If they truly believe in me, in themselves, and in

Wakan-Tanka and the Helpers, my hand will usually become very hot. But if they do not believe in any one or all of us, it will usually become very cold. My hand is never wrong. Sometimes though, the feeling is not as distinct as I would like it to be, so then I wrap up in my black cloth to learn what their faith really is."

"Do you just lay your hand on their shoulder?" I asked, because I thought I had detected movement as he did it.

"No," he answered, "I rub the shoulder gently so they will know the love I have for them. I care about them, even if some people don't

have enough faith, and it makes me cry to learn this and to have to send them away."

The lump in my throat had subsided by now, but his compassion almost brought it back. I needed to keep talking to prevent it, and I turned the conversation to a matter he had mentioned — that of wrapping up to learn things about a patient from *Wakan-Tanka* and the Helpers.

In *Teton Sioux Music,* Frances Densmore records an account given by Used-as-a-Shield, "a reliable informant," in which he tells how a medicine man treated him for an undisclosed illness, after which he recovered and was well again. During this treatment, one of the things the medicine man did was to "take out a black cloth, which he tied over his eyes."[58] He then continued the treatment, with no explanation being given in the account as to what happened to him once the black cloth was tied on. Here again we find that Fools Crow carried on another ancient tradition, for he commonly wrapped a black cloth over his eyes as he began to work with a patient — the difference between his account and that of Densmore being that Fools Crow told me why he did this, and what happened when he did.

It was fairly common to arrive at Fools Crow's house, find a visitor's automobile there, and have a relative of Fools Crow tell you that "Grandpa is wrapped up." You knew then that Fools Crow had put on his black cloth and was treating the visitor. Often too, when Fools Crow and I were alone and working on the book a patient would arrive. Once he had decided to proceed, Fools Crow would wrap up to begin his work with the patient. Whenever he traveled, and especially when it was to see a patient, he took the black cloth and his collection of stones, herbs and roots with him, and wrapped up to learn some of the things he needed to know.

The black cloth Fools Crow used for curing was about four inches wide and five feet long. The ends were split so they could be tucked in or tied. At the time I saw it, the edges were frayed from long use, and the cloth itself was well worn, but there were no holes in it. He let me hold the cloth, and he even put it on me to show me

---

[58] Densmore, 1918, pp. 247-248.

how effective it was in shutting out the light. But he did not, during the months we were together, ever put this cloth on anyone else, and only Kate and a couple of close friends were allowed to wrap it on him. To Fools Crow, the cloth was a sacred item.

One day, I asked him where he obtained the cloth, and he told me his first one was given to him by Stirrup, along with instructions for its use. When the original one finally wore out, he replaced it with the present one. It was Fools Crow's intention to pass this cloth on to some worthy medicine person, but I doubted that he would have the opportunity to do this. (As indicated in Chapter 1, his medicine bundle may have been passed on to someone else and is apparently lost.)

The matter of the black wrapping and its use led to several discussions regarding darkness in its relationship to curing, healing, and prophetic work. "Why," I asked, "do you wrap up, and why is darkness so often a part of what you do?"

His hands went up. "To reach full communion with *Wakan-Tanka* and the Helpers, I must isolate myself from all distractions, including intruding thoughts, and create a quiet place where I am fully open to Them and focused on the matter at hand. The black cloth enables me to do this in a very effective way. Darkness also allows my mind's eye to take over, because it can see far beyond what my physical eyes can see. Have you noticed that images stand out very well against a dark background? When the wrapping is on me, my senses are keener and come alive. Darkness helps what I feel and sharpens my hearing for spiritual sounds. Even whispers become like shouts. And if a patient is with me in the darkness, such as when we are both standing under the same blanket, we are floating around in a mood that makes us think of spiritual things and the Higher Powers. Then we are more open to Them. These are just some of the reasons why I and some of the other medicine people sometimes cure or heal at night, and why the vision quester's greatest visions usually come to them at night. Sun is good, and light is good. But during the daytime we see with our physical eyes and it is harder to concentrate on spiritual matters. The different ways are ways *Wakan-Tanka* and the Helpers have given me to use for different situations."

"And how do you learn whether wrapping up or using a blanket will be best in a given situation?"

"When the gifts were given to me I was told which would work best for certain things. The blanket is not used as often, but it is especially useful in cases of heavy bleeding."

Fools Crow sometimes wrapped his black cloth on himself, but more often it was done by Kate. It was wide enough to cover his eyes, and part of his nose and forehead. His simplest approach was to form a small altar on the ground by marking the four corners with cloths of the Directional colors. He then laid a bed of sage in the middle of the cloths and stood on the middle of the bed while the black cloth was wrapped on him. Then he prayed, asking for the help and guidance of *Wakan-Tanka* and the Helpers, and in a short while was shown by his stone or his mind-screen what the problem was, what caused it, what medicine to use, and how to prepare and apply it. Remember that this was only one of the ways he had for diagnosing. The others are described elsewhere.

In *Fools Crow*, I describe the curing he did for a patient who was suffering from mental illness. In this instance, he put a black cloth hood over his own head, and another hood over the head of the patient (In Chapter 12, you will find that two hoods are also used as part of the healing treatment). Assistants closed the curtains to darken the room Fools Crow and the patient were in. After singing his song, the holy man saw sparks coming out of the top of the man's head, and afterward came little worms with red heads. The rest of the people in the room did not see the sparks or worms, but with the spirits' help, Fools Crow did, and the treatment he was given cured the patient.[59]

On three occasions, I saw him use the blanket covering and learned that his usual method was to build a tiny fire outdoors, and to feed it with scrapings from a large buffalo horn. This provided the sweet smell needed to draw the Higher Powers close and the sweetened smoke to carry up the prayers being said or sung. The coals of the fire established the center of an altar that was formed by placing four colored cloths around it. This altar was large enough for the

---

[59] *Fools Crow*, 1979, p. 150.

patient to stand on one side facing the fire, and for Fools Crow to stand on the other side of the fire and facing the person. An assistant, usually Kate, then threw an ordinary blanket, not a star quilt, over both of them and adjusted it until they were completely covered and all light was shut out, except that provided by the smoldering coals. When the blanket was used, Fools Crow did not touch the patient at any time. He simply sang his song very softly and did certain rituals.

> HO!
> We stand together in the darkness.
> Here too is the spirit of the buffalo.
> It still helps us.
> It provided everything.
> It still helps us.
> You over there, it will make you well.
> *Wakan-Tanka* will see our thanks.

It should be noted here that Fools Crow never spoke of "hearing our thanks." It was always, "see our thanks," the important thing being that he had learned that we must do something and live in such a way that *Wakan-Tanka* and the Helpers will see our thanksgiving in action. Spoken thanks are too easily given, and too easily forgotten.

Immediately after the song, Fools Crow did one of two things: the first was to light an herb on the coals at his feet, and then to use his hands to toss the smoke from it toward the patient, who was instructed to inhale it deeply, and if possible without coughing. The second was to hold a feather in his right hand that was pointed toward the patient, and to blow his breath across the feather. In the curings being described, the patients were told to bathe their faces, heads, necks and chests with the breath.

"How did you know which treatment to use in a given instance?" I asked.

"I looked up at my mind-screen," he replied, "and did visioning."

"Which way did you use for the woman who had internal bleeding?"

"I tossed the smoke to her with my hands."

"What did you see then, and what happened with the bleeding?"

"I already told you," he replied. (This remark was a reference to what he previously told of the incident in the *Fools Crow* book.) "I said a prayer about slowing the blood down and kept it up until the blood stopped. I looked into the patient with my stone and saw this

happen. I also saw it on my mind-screen. Sometimes I use both the stone and the screen to make sure. I saw drops of blood, first slowing down and then stopping completely. This is a thing anyone can do to control bleeding, either for themselves or for someone else."

I was to remember what Fools Crow had said about slowing down bleeding when I met a young woman who attended a workshop of mine in Tulsa, Oklahoma, in 1988. She told me she had learned that bleeding could be stopped by mind control, and that she had in fact done it herself on two occasions when she had had major surgeries for malignant tumors. Each time, and before she was anesthetized, she made her dubious surgeon promise to tell her to shut down her internal bleeding. The surgeon kept the promise and was astonished when the bleeding slowed immediately to a trickle. This same young woman also applied the idea to the recovery process. She programmed herself to recover quickly and with a minimum of pain. In both instances, she awakened within half an hour, felt remarkably good, and insisted that she be returned to her room.

In the first book, Fools Crow describes in considerable detail how he treated a woman for an irregular heart beat. This was done inside a house. The living room floor was cleared of furniture, and he made a small altar on it by spreading out a square bed of sage and placing a piece of colored cloth at each of four corners. The orientation of the altar was south and north, and at the south end he laid down side-by-side four golden-eagle feathers, with their tips pointed toward the west.[60]

The woman removed her shoes and stood barefooted on the center of the altar. Besides Fools Crow, there were four singers present, two of whom had drums, and the two others rattles.

Fools Crow smudged the woman and everyone else, including himself. Thus purified, he sang his song four times, and held his pipe horizontally in his hands while he was wrapped up. The shades were drawn and the lights were turned out. The singers then played and sang their rain song. At its end, there was a clap of thunder so powerful it shook the house, and even though the sky outside was clear, a wet mist filled the room. Fools Crow gave this song to me, but explained that it was not the exact song which was sung by the singers, and for the same reasons previously given.

> We are calling You.
> It will rain plenty.
> Everything is growing.
> Feathers are making air.
> Everything is moving.
> The Persons are moving.
> Ho, we see them!

Fools Crow handed the pipe to the woman, and knowing what to do with it, she held it stem first out toward the Directions as she slowly turned in a clockwise direction until she had made the full

---

[60] See also *Fools Crow*, p. 205.

circle four times. When she was done, the lights were turned on, and Fools Crow removed his wrapping. He told the woman that he had been shown the cause of the problem, and what medicine he was to use. She was to return the next morning at 8 a.m., and treatment would begin. This consisted of boiling an herb in water to make a tea which he gave her to drink at two hour intervals, four times a day for four days. During the treatments he talked softly to her to comfort and calm her. At the end she was entirely at peace, no longer anxious or afraid, and felt much better.

"Tell me more about this treatment," I said. "What happens when you are wrapped up there and in the dark?"

"I see the four feathers fluttering, and I know that the power is present and in motion. Then I focus my mind on the pieces of colored cloth. Pretty soon, one of them will float into the air, and will begin to circle around the person. After awhile, it will stop and touch the person. The place where it does this is where the problem is. In this case, the color of the north, red, which has to do with health, rose up and finally settled on her just over her heart. I looked into her there, and saw her heart beating in a crazy fashion. I prayed to the North, and on my mind-screen I was shown which medicine to use to cure her. It was one I already had in my medicine bundle. I used it, and when the four days of treatment were done, she was well."

"Why do the feathers point toward the west?"

"Because that is where the Thunder Being lives. Everyone there heard him answer. He sent cleansing water and prepared the woman for healing."

"Is this treatment only used for certain illnesses?"

"It is one of those given to me to use for people who can move around (are mobile). I have one like it for those who can not move. I told you about the man who was brought to me who was paralyzed.[61] For him I made an altar like the one for the woman, except that it was long enough to lay the person down on. Generally, I do the same things then that I did for the woman, and the same things happen. I always make a tea for the person to drink. One thing that is different

[61] *Fools Crow,* 1979, pp. 202-203.

is that I have a pepper-like plant medicine I rub on the person's body. I grind up the leaves, roots, and stems, and then rub the powder on him. I might make a liquid with it. In either case, it stimulates them and makes them want to move."

"Does one of the Directional cloths move in this instance also?"

"Yes."

"What determines which one?"

"The Helpers. The Person in that Direction not only tells me where the cause and problems are, He tells me which Persons I am to call in when I talk with the patients as I am healing them. They tell me what to emphasize; what the patient needs to hear most. It is their decision, and they know better than I do what is best."

"Is a person's illness always a mystery? It seems that sick or injured people usually know where they are hurting."

Fools Crow shoved that statement away with a flip of his hand. "Even the white doctors push and probe to find out all they can about a patient's problem — just how bad and how big it is. It is true that patients usually know where it hurts. They come holding their throats or stomach or something else. But that does not tell me everything I need to know about it, or what the cause is. I need to know what the cause is, because I have to cure both. If I just cure the illness without curing the cause, the illness might come back. This is where the wrapping-up comes in, where using my stone, my mind-screen or my crystal helps me. They are my x-ray machines and more, since they show me the injury, its complications, the cause, and if I don't know already, how to treat it. If necessary, they even show me new things I haven't been taught before. I have visited many hospital patients, and I have been a patient in the hospital here at Pine Ridge a few times. I think the white doctors could use their mind-screens and some crystals, because there is plenty they don't seem to know or be able to do."

Dallas chuckled, for he had been in the reservation hospitals too and I knew had some negative thoughts about them. For anything complex, Sioux patients had to be sent to Denver, Colorado, or to Lincoln, Nebraska. But I had mixed feelings about Fools Crow's assertion. I knew that the Public Health doctors at Pine Ridge and Rosebud worked in poorly supplied and deteriorating facilities and at times handled overwhelming case loads. It was not surprising that the Sioux harbored negative opinions about the accomplishments of the hospitals. During the years I visited there, the general word among the traditional Indians was that the hospitals were "places where people go to die." In more than one instance, when Fools Crow was moved into certain hospital rooms that were suspect, he simply got out of bed, put his clothes on, walked out of the hospital, and went home. He was afraid that if he didn't do it then, he never would.

Enjoying the levity that his statement had aroused in Dallas, who was laughing heartily, Fools Crow added, "Maybe we should take the doctors some black cloths and blankets — if they don't mind using some with holes in them. That's the only kind we have."

"How did you happen to be in the hospital?" I asked.

"My relatives took me there when I had fainted or was too weak to resist."

"Could you have healed yourself?"

"In those instances, I never had a chance to find out."

"How about other times, did you do it then?"

He looked me straight in the eye and said, "I am eighty-seven years old; how do you think I got here?"

"I knew you did self-healing," I said with a smile, "I just wanted you to say it. When you self-heal, do you also treat yourself four times a day for four days?"

"Always. Even if I feel all right in a shorter time, I continue the treatments. That is the way I was taught to do it. I've noticed too that every time a doctor gives me pills, he tells me to take all of them, even if I am feeling good after I have taken only half."

"And do you take the pills?"

"Sometimes yes, sometimes no. I know that all pills do is start the body doing what is necessary for curing. The tools *Wakan-Tanka* has given me can do that better than the pills can."

It was late in the evening. I was hungry, and I nudged the conversation away from hospitals and pills, and back to some unfinished business. "Do you usually spend four days treating a patient who is paralyzed?" I asked. "That would be difficult for them, and for those who had to bring them to you."

"The paralyzed man I just mentioned stayed with me for four days. But you have seen that in my curings, *Wakan-Tanka* makes adjustments for each situation. If, for example, a patient cannot drink tea, I apply the medicine in another way, such as rubbing it on them with my hands. Also, you have seen me do curings without any preparation at all, such as the time at the Sun Dance when I straightened that boy's twisted leg. There is no fixed way for *Wakan-Tanka* and the Helpers to heal. They do what is best, and what will work, and I do not ask them questions about it. As I said before, that is for white people to do."

11 BASKETS OF LOVE

MANY OF THE WAYS FOOLS CROW WAS GIVEN FOR CURING HAVE already been described, but we still needed to discuss his general approach to the matter of curing, and also the specific medicines he used. In adding this material to what has already been considered, the variety of ways he was given to cure will become even more apparent, and again raise the question of, "Why so many?" Fools Crow has explained the diversity by saying it was because *Wakan-Tanka* knew that different things would work with different people, and the Higher Powers did not want the task to be more arduous than it already was for the hollow bones who were involved in the curing. The Powers maintained excitement and heightened the challenge by varying the ways and the pace. The unexpected was an ever-present possibility, and from beginning to end curing remained an adventure. There was always something new to use, and there were always new mountains to conquer. At the same time, all of this was undergirded with assurance. There was the inner knowing that the same God had taught the same things to people the world over.

There were the firm promises of success that *Wakan-Tanka* and the Helpers had given, and which had been fulfilled countless times. The central parts of every curing way were rooted in ancient teachings that had proven their worth over the centuries. The combatants entered the fray firmly believing they would win, and they knew that even death was, for those who understood the ultimate purpose of life, a victory.

Except for the variations I have noted, a customary and natural routine was followed with every patient, and I repeat here that while I am using the word "patient," and have even put it into Fools Crow's mouth, he never did use it. He referred to those who came to him as a "person," or more preferably by name. He intuitively knew that calling someone a patient did something negative to their sense of personal worth, and that it impaired and weakened the otherwise

strong relationship between his patients and himself — a relationship that he considered essential to success.

The routine was as follows, and it was used for self-curing and curing. I number its steps for clarity for presentation, but Fools Crow would have moaned over the idea of numbering anything that was done in and through him by *Wakan-Tanka* and the Helpers. Numbering would take away the softness and the mystery — with the Higher Powers all things merged and became part of whole. How could they be divided up? Only white people (which, of course, is what I am) would do that. At the same time, Fools Crow would be the first to admit that the steps were, exceptions noted, vital to success. Given time and opportunity to do a full ceremony correctly, it must be done so. And, the routine itself was a way of gathering power in, stirring power up, and setting power into motion. The way was old. The way was proven. Why vary it? He did not understand the passion we have for wanting to add something or to reshape everything to make it our own, although he understood that we are always given an opportunity to enter in by applying the old ways to present situations and needs. Of course, for Him, just the service was enough. Anything else would be, in our way of expressing it, "gravy" or "dessert."

Step 1. The person must bring an offering of tobacco to Fools Crow. In the early days, this was supposed to be specially grown and mixed sacred tobacco brought in a pipe. But as years passed and the sacred tobacco became harder to procure, he began to accept commercial products in cigarette, or loose form which he himself would fashion into a cigarette. Why tobacco? Because *Wakan-Tanka* has put sacramental power into it. The sweet smell of it tells you that. And because the smoke from it carries prayers and requests up to Him. Smoke is related to fire. "It comes out of it." And fire is very sacred. Therefore the smoking is the actual beginning of the curing process. And if the smoking is not done, the process will not begin. When tobacco is smoked, it must be smoked in its entirety to signify that the treatment will be thoroughly done and thoroughly effective.

Step 2. Once the tobacco was brought, Fools Crow had to know whether or not he should smoke it. This was determined by his measuring the faith of the person. "How big was it?" The way of doing this has been described, but it included looking into the person with the mind's eye, and as he did so rubbing his hand on the patient's shoulder to see whether it would grow hot or cold. Fools Crow did absolutely nothing to influence what happened to the hand. "If I influenced it," he said, "who would I be fooling by making it go the way I wanted it to? I might be curing something that did not need to be cured, I would not truly have *Wakan-Tanka's* help, and I would be deceiving the person who trusted me."

Step 3. Once the tobacco was smoked, Fools Crow talked with the person for a long time about the way of curing. He patiently explained that what he would do had its roots in ancient history. The way that *Wakan-Tanka* would use was old and proven. Fools Crow himself had used all of his methods many times with great success. The person was going to see this happen in his own life now. It would be exciting, and the community would see the person healthy again and know that *Wakan-Tanka* was watching over the people. *"Waste, waste, waste,"* Fools Crow would say, "Good, good, good!" As the person's confidence and hope started to grow, Fools Crow talked with the person about the cause of the illness, what had happened since it started, who the person had already gone to for help, and what had been done. As they talked, Fools Crow sifted through the answers and compared the situation to others he had treated that were like it. In particular, he wanted to know whether the illness was related to another person or persons, whether someone in the family had it, and especially whether bad relationships were contributing to the degree in which the illness was affecting the person. How also, he would ask, was the person's illness affecting his family?

A very special thing Fools Crow did was to remind people that the ancient and proven way was to do the treatment four times a day, at four equal intervals a day, for four days. Four was a sacred number and had power in itself. The treatments would build in intensity. While he would do the same things during each treatment, he would start slowly and each time do them a little faster, press a little harder, talk more about success and hope. The main thing he would do while he was applying medicine would be to lead his patients into a deep sense of peace, which, Fools Crow would tell them, is "freedom from fear." Since *Wakan-Tanka* and the Helpers were the real curers, they would be present in and through Fools Crow, and there was no limit to what they could achieve. By the time the last treatment was applied on the fourth day, the people's anticipation would be at a fever pitch. They would be ready, and what they hoped for would happen. After the treatments had ended, the Higher Powers would continue to walk with the people, not only until they were entirely healthy, but ever afterwards. "Know this, and claim it," the holy man would say.

The entire purpose of this lengthy discussion was to draw the people completely into the curing process, to engage their total persons, to get them communing fully with *Wakan-Tanka* and the Helpers, and to enhance their own curing abilities and those of the "hollow bones" who treated them. Consequently, they set into motion both cure and success as their minds dispatched the curing agents to where they were needed by the body and evicted both the cause and the illness.

Step 4. Fools Crow wrapped up, or used a stone and blanket, or went into the Purifications Lodge to determine all he could about the illness. He added what he learned to what the person had already told him. He learned both the specifics and the full magnitude of the problem. He also learned what medicines he should use, and how he should apply them. He let the Higher Powers have both a continuing and a final say in which way to go.

Step 5. As the treatments got underway, Fools Crow opened himself fully to *Wakan-Tanka* and the Helpers to call in curing power. As the days passed, he became more and more engrossed in the process and, in truth, forgot himself in the sense that nothing else mattered. He tolerated no interruptions and did not, even for a moment, turn aside for anything else. If he needed to go to the bathroom, he did it between treatments, and preferably before he started in the morning or at the end of a day.

He concentrated upon "touching with his eyes" and communicating to the person his profound love. "The person has to feel this," he told me. "They have to know that everything that I am doing is being sent to them in a basket of love. Then, when it has reached them, their own love for me will begin to grow. Watch closely, and sometimes during the four days you will see them reach out and touch me on the cheek or the shoulder. (Once God had given me eyes to see, I saw this happen many times.) Then I know their love is as big as mine. When the curing is done, we remain lovers for the rest of our lives. We are closer than brothers and sisters, we are one in *Wakan-Tanka*. This love has nothing to do with physical things, it has to do with unity of heart and spirit and mind."

Step 6. To deepen this communication of love, Fools Crow applied his medicines gently, and sometimes would sing or hum "sound songs" as he worked. His hands moved gracefully, and gestures accompanied everything he did. Usually, he did things in four moves, that is, if he was using an herb to make an application of medicine, he would move it toward the person and back three times before he actually applied it the fourth time. A feather would be used in the same way, and a cup of tea would only be held up to the person's lips on the fourth pass. It must be emphasized that the use of the sacred numbers four or seven was part of building confidence. The person believed that these numbers in themselves had spiritual power, and when anything was done in 4s or 7s, their spiritual power was added to the spiritual power of whatever else was being done. This magnified the power in an interesting way, because it was not a $1 + 1 = 2$ equation, it was a $1 + 1 = 10$, or 20, or 30. The sum was determined not by simple mathematics, but by the faith of the people involved — holy man and person together. The greater the faith, the greater the result. Cherokee prayer formulas were designed to work in this same way. Their parts consisted of statements made in combinations of sacred numbers, and what the formulas accomplished was greatly magnified because people believed that was what would happen when they used them.

Step 7. When the treatment ended, thanks must be offered to *Wakan-Tanka* and the Helpers, and the promises must be claimed. The latter is what people most often fail to do, and because of this the effect of the curing can be short-lived. Fools Crow had his patients accomplish this in the traditional way, by insisting that during the four days following the fourth day of curing they deny themselves things that mean something. He would join them by denying himself things, and he would remind them that this is what the pledgers did after every Sun Dance ended. One suggestion he would make is that they fast part of the time. Usually he would be in a good mood by now and tell them that fasting would not be too great a problem, since, unemployment being what it was (higher than eighty percent at Pine Ridge today), and government rations being what they were, they fasted most of the time anyway. (I personally recall Charles Ross telling me that during the holdout at Wounded Knee in 1973 the FBI sent word that if the Indians didn't give up, they were going to surround the place and shut off all of their food supplies. The Indians replied, "Why don't you do something we aren't used to!") So along with fasting, Fools Crow advised the cured persons to deny themselves sex, social activities, and, if they had it, television. They were also to go apart with their pipes, reflect upon the blessings they had received, and spend as much time as possible thanking the Higher Powers. They should purify themselves regularly, and learn to think of themselves as hollow bones.

Also, they should not talk overly much about what had happened to them, and certainly must not brag about it. What had transpired was a unique and personal thing between *Wakan-Tanka*, the Helpers, Fools Crow, and themselves. To share it or to brag about it would spoil that. Of course, other people should see by the way the cured people lived now that their faith was rooted in the Higher Powers, and whenever the opportunity arose they would encourage others to share this faith.

What I have described thus far in this chapter pertains to four-day rituals. Exceptions to this were the Purifications Lodge and Yuwipi ceremonies, which were one-time events where patients were concerned. There might be follow-up instructions for the patients and medicines to take, but the Purifications Lodge and Yuwipi ceremonies themselves were not repeated. Nevertheless, these two ways of treating patients may be the most powerful in terms of what they achieve. Certainly, Fools Crow's Purifications Lodge rite where *Wakan-Tanka* himself actually came to do the curing has to be placed at the top of the list.

Besides the "sound songs" Fools Crow used while he was curing, he also had his own healing song. Although I heard it many times and know precisely how it went, it was a song that he did not feel free to reveal. It was too personal and memorable for that. But he did disclose the essence of its parts so that I can pass them along, and in communion with *Wakan-Tanka* those who wish to can build on these their own curing songs.[62] Please remember that each line of the song ended with Fools Crow's personal "whoo, whoo" sound, done in a gentle and affectionate way.

Line 1. He asked *Wakan-Tanka* to help him cure the person.

Line 2. He asked Grandmother Earth to help him cure the person.

Line 3. He appealed to the Directions, to the Day and the Night and the Seasons, to send their individual powers to help him cure the person.

Line 4. He told the Ones he had addressed that his wish was for the person to walk with straight limbs, be healthy, have a good heart, and have love for other people.

Line 5. He described the person being healed as his friend.

Line 6. The song was concluded by asking the Higher Powers to help the person by returning him to good health.

Line 7. He expressed thanks in advance for the success he knew would come.

Notice that the entire thrust of the song is positive. There is no hint of, or opening for, failure. When we consider the seven steps that are followed for successful curing, it is evident that the person being healed is drawn mentally and physically into the struggle against his illness. More than anything else, it can be called an engagement of the mind, which we know today can exercise great influence over the body's response to illness. The approach can be seen even more clearly as we observe that between each of the daily treatments the patient is directed to make use of the sacred hoop to ask *Wakan-Tanka* and the Helpers to help him examine himself, and to regenerate his spirits in the areas the Persons in the Four Directions can help him with: rebirth, renewal, procreation and thanksgiving.

Those who were Native American already knew how to make the hoop, and probably brought their own with them to the curing sessions. Those who did not were shown how to make it and told

---

[62] You can find this same information about the song on page 205 of *Fools Crow*.

how to use it. The typical fourteen-inch diameter hoop and its appendages are illustrated here. It is made of willow and has directional strings and colored cloth patches attached. Its main use is to help the patients review themselves and their lives, and to reflect upon their relationship to their people and to *Wakan-Tanka* and the Helpers.

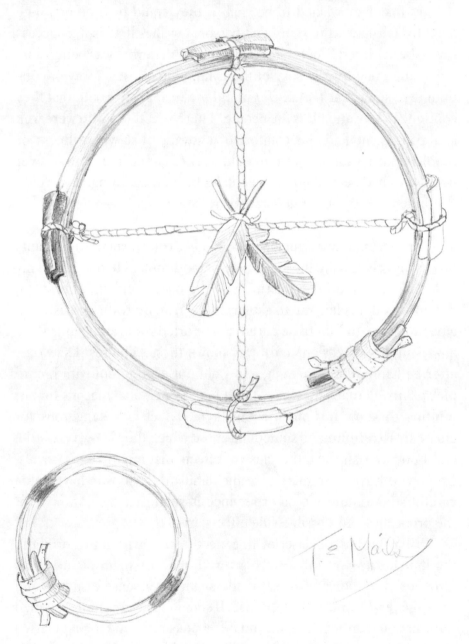

After the final treatment each day patients had dinner, and from then until bedtime were directed to spend time in quiet meditation about their relationship with *Wakan-Tanka*. The meditation involved deep breathing and prayer, with the prayer consisting of both petition and listening. Above all, the patients were to emphasize in their prayers that they wished to be well so they could help others. The need for curing had to transcend personal wishes if a lasting success was to be achieved. Fools Crow emphasized that what was being done was being done for the sake of the community. It was a way of continuing to show that *Wakan-Tanka* and the Helpers live, and that they continue to love and bless the people. Therefore, those who were well at the moment had the comfort of knowing that when illness or problems struck them, they too could be cured or healed. The Answer was there, had been there for centuries beyond counting, and would continue to be there for generations to come.

As every medicine person does, Fools Crow learned to use plants for curing; employing the leaves, stems, and roots. He did not, to my knowledge, keep a huge pharmacy of the plants on hand, but went, or better said was led, out to gather these on an individual basis when a person came to him to be cured. Some dried roots and plants were always in his possession, and I was shown these. The rest I saw only after he had brought them in, and I did not ever go out with him to pick plants. Perhaps he sensed that I had my personal reasons for not wanting to know too much about them. I feel it is dangerous for amateurs to recommend something about which they know very little, and I do not wish to be the cause of effects that might be disastrous. I prefer to leave such matters in the hands of those who have made careful studies, and whose experience is such that they know what the properties and possible side effects are.

What I will do is describe in general terms, without resorting to the individual names that were given to me, the main plants Fools Crow used for curing, so that readers can get a sense of these, and of the general scope of his expertise. If someone desires more detailed information than this, the old and new books referring to plants used for curing are numerous and readily available in bookstores and libraries. Once again though, I advise caution. While there is much to recommend in the use of plants that the Native Americans themselves employed, I urge that they only be utilized with professional guidance. An excellent guide book to be recommended in this regard is *Natural Health, Natural Medicine — A Comprehensive Manual For Wellness And Self-Care,* by Andrew Weil, M.D. It is published by Houghton Mifflin Company, Boston, 1990.

Comparing Fools Crow's pharmacy with that of Frances Densmore's Sioux informants, I would say that he used most of the same plants that the author was told about and shown, and he had others besides. Fools Crow traveled to other Sioux reservations to obtain certain plants, and to the reservations of other tribes. He even went on occasion to the Black Hills and the Rocky Mountains. He always stored up some for winter use, since the ground in South Dakota is usually covered for months with a deep blanket of snow and ice.

His customary method of application was to boil either one or several parts of the plant in a bucket or basin that was partially filled with water. The boiling was done on a stove or over an outside fire, shortly after he had completed his morning prayer — which was done daily just at sunrise. If no patient was being treated, he prayed again after lunch, and a final time at sundown. In total, anywhere from three to six hours would be consumed in prayer, and the more he had to accomplish the more he prayed. I've already explained why.

Some of the broth was set aside to cool, and timed to be ready when the person arrived for treatment. Enough was prepared to last for the four treatments of that day. The person was given either a cup or a glassfull to drink, and the amount of the plant part that was put in the water varied. Sometimes it was so powerful that only a pinch would do. Other roots, leaves and stems might be dumped in the water in copious amounts. Fools Crow either had been taught by Stirrup or was guided by the Higher Powers as to how much of each plant to use. Sometimes a root was given to the person to chew, and other times it might be lighted and the smoke from it would either be blown four times or wafted with a feather in four moves toward the person, who in either case would bathe himself in it. Some herbs had sprigs that were like little brushes, and these might be used to "paint" the medicine on the person's skin. I saw Fools Crow do this to remove disfiguring birthmarks from the faces of two men, and the result in both instances was immediate and spectacular. At the end of the fourth treatment on the fourth day, he dropped the sprig, clapped his hands smartly together, and the birth marks were gone! In case someone is wondering, there was no thought transference involved in this. I sat there, I saw it, and Fools Crow did not appear in ancient clothing. Afterwards, one of the men married and his wife bore him two children. I saw him several times when I returned to the reservation, and his face remained perfectly clear.

It is important to know that Fools Crow believed successful curing was a combination of the Higher Powers, the medicine person, medicine, and procedure. Spiritual power was the infusing and leavening ingredient. None of the individual participants would accomplish a full cure without the others. Their separate powers combined to achieve the required potency. Mood enhancers were also beneficial. Fire, sage, sweetgrass, and music made their contributions. Support from family and friends was essential, and their attitudes must be of a kind that encouraged the patient to focus upon life and living. Even the locale where the curing was done played its role. The better the setting, the more profound the results, and the quicker they were achieved. Sometimes the kind of illness called for treatment at night, in a darkened room, or in the darkened Purifications Lodge, where a heightened mood of *Wakan-Tanka's* presence could be achieved. I did not see Fools Crow treat a person outside at night, but he told me he sometimes did, and that he knew medicine men who did it regularly with good success.

Fools Crow rejected any suggestion that the medicines used by the Sioux were arrived at by a trial and error process. To him, that would be the same as saying that the best *Wakan-Tanka* could do for humans was to leave them to their own devices, or that perhaps there really was no "Power" to help anyway; that *Wakan-Tanka* existed only in the imaginations of primitive and superstitious peoples. Furthermore, a trial and error process would imply that *Wakan-Tanka* did not care enough about the people He created to provide guidance for them over the centuries, and that He just left them to suffer and die until the trial and error process was completed.

"To accept such a thing," the old holy man said, "makes the Higher Powers ogres rather than loving Beings. I, and all other medicine people, have been and are led by *Wakan-Tanka* and the Helpers to the plants that we need for healing. Just as They are involved in all of the curing ways, so too They are involved in choosing the plants. What I use from my medicine bundle or get from the fields and forests is not an accidental thing. I use many medicines, yet I have never given a person a medicine that has made them more ill, or has even caused a side-effect. Only the medicines of white doctors do that. They give us prescriptions as if the same thing will work the same way in everyone. Only after the person gets worse do they look for another pill or another way. Many times they mix different pills and medicines together, and there is no way they can know what is going to happen. Well, no matter what anyone has reported, this does not happen to us. Sometimes in the past people died shortly after being given medicines, but who can say that, already being close to death, they died from the medicine? White cemeteries are full of people that have gone to doctors too. We are a small tribe, yet we have big cemeteries here at Pine Ridge and Rosebud, and most of the people that are buried in them came from the Public Health hospitals, not from holy or medicine men like myself. After all, most of our people have for a long time been persuaded not to come to us for treatment. Someday though, everyone will realize that the best kind of treatment for everyone in the world is to combine the center (essence) of what we do with what the white doctors do. Then the cures will be truly great."[63]

"Knowing the general attitude of medical people," I commented, "I wonder whether this can really happen."

Fools Crow stood up and walked around while he answered, and I could see that he wanted me to listen carefully to what he was about

---

[63] It should be noted that in recent years, what Fools Crow recommends has begun. Some (although not nearly enough) hospitals are asking medicine persons to share in the curing process for Indians. Fools Crow would tell every hospital to expand the use of medicine persons to include every patient. When you examine the basic principals he employed in his curing, it is not so naive a suggestion as one might expect . . . not commercially lucrative perhaps, but assuredly more helpful to the "humanity" of human beings.

to say. "White people," he said, "talk about the strange costumes our medicine men used to wear, and about the strange things they did as they jumped around and growled like animals. Those who find these actions to be primitive fail to understand how the costumes and the actions helped the patient's attitude about life and living. They responded to what was done in a positive way."

"You are talking about the psychology involved in curing," I said.

"Ho," Fools Crow replied. "I know that big word, psychology, but it is a hard one for me to say and we have no word for it in Lakota."

One of Fools Crow's favorite plants was what he called "dock." He used its leaves and powdered root to make a poultice or a salve to treat skin problems and to stop bleeding. It was applied to boils and burns. It also reduced arthritis, rheumatism, bruises and swellings. When made into a tea, dock reduced fevers, helped kidney problems, and treated sore throats, constipation, and diarrhea.

When he was invited on one occasion to the Crow reservation in Montana to treat a person, a Crow medicine woman gave him information about a chokecherry tea that was useful in treating colds, skin problems, mumps, lice, and throat and chest problems.

For open wounds, he had his patients chew a dried plant he obtained in the Bad Lands. Some of the chewed pulp was also spread on the wound.

Another chewed root cured mouth and tooth problems, and was also good for a sore throat.

For rattlesnake bites he boiled the leaves and stem of a plant and made them into a poultice that both relieved the pain and drew out some of the poison.

For people who had run into poison ivy, Fools Crow had a plant whose stems and leaves were ground into a powder that was sprinkled on the afflicted areas.

For people who had lost their appetite, Fools Crow used the root of a certain plant that grew along the creek banks. This was dried, crumbled, placed in water, and boiled to make a tea.

For headaches, he had patients steam their faces over the coals in the Purifications Lodge. If a lodge was not available, he had them cover their heads and face with a towel and stand over a boiling tea made from the roots, stems and leaves of another plant that grew near creeks. Out in the flat areas there was an herb whose root was dried, ground to a powder, and then sprinkled on hot coals so that a patient with a bad cough could inhale the fumes.

There was a certain plant that was used by bears and grew in wooded areas. Fools Crow learned about this one from Stirrup, and he employed it to treat swollen limbs and broken, fractured, or twisted bones. Its dried leaves and root were mixed with bear grease. Usually, he warmed his greased hands over hot coals and then rubbed the skin over the injured areas. In the *Fools Crow* book I reported the occasion at a Sun Dance where he straightened the twisted leg of a young boy. But I omitted until now the fact that he used this plant when he did it. I also saw him use it with success on the aching and swollen legs of two white nurses.

A certain root bears used was ground up and made into a tea that relieved bowel pains. This one Fools Crow told me he learned about by watching bears, but I doubt that he had any way of knowing what their exact problem was. He must have tested the root, and found out what it would do.

Bear berries, their stems and leaves, were ground together and then boiled in water to make a tea Fools Crow used to treat kidney problems, and the back pains that were associated with them.

Fevers were treated in two ways. One way was to steep a certain herb by pouring warm water over it. Some of the brew was drunk by the person, and some of it was rubbed on the person's body. Another way was to crush and boil the blossoms of a different plant to make a tea.

Both internal and external bleeding was treated with a tea made from an herb that was found in damp creek beds. This was another one that was given to Fools Crow by Stirrup. The stalks and leaves of the same plant made a tea whose drops soothed pains, such as those of an earache. Fools Crow told me that among his people this was a very old remedy, and upon checking I found it in Densmore's *Teton Sioux Music* material, page 264.

Stirrup also passed on to Fools Crow information about an herb that would cause people with food poisoning to vomit. The herb was chewed and then spewed onto the back of the neck and head. Fools

Crow chuckled when he told me about it, and said that he never knew whether it was the herb or the fact of its being spewed on the person that made the person throw up.

Fools Crow had a certain berry that he obtained in Crow country. He dried this and ground it up, then mixed the powder with warm water to make a tea that helped people's appetites.

He had a leafed plant that grew out in the flat areas. It was dried, boiled, and made into a tea that people who had kidney problems drank at same time they ate food.

I will say again that what I report here is not Fools Crow's entire pharmacy, although I believe it represents the greater part. All I wish to do in any case is to show that his curing practice was as extensive as he declared a holy person's would be. He claimed that he could cure virtually everything, and the wide range of what he did supports the claim. In his last years before he ceased to practice regularly, he even treated cancer with success, although the next chapter shows there were some reservations regarding what he did. Other than this, the list of people and different illnesses that were treated in and through him is unparalleled. Something that should be noted in connection with these claims is that he reports in the *Fools Crow* book virtually all of the names of the people whose cures are described. So, if his assertions were not true, they could be easily contested. But the *Fools Crow* book has been on the market for eleven years now, and no one has stepped forward to do this. Also, in many of the reported instances, I and others were there to witness them, and I do not think we are particularly gullible people. Until I met Fools Crow and other medicine men and women, I felt that I was well named — "Thomas" — for I fitted the nature of the Thomas that had to see with his own eyes the wounds of Jesus before he would believe. Now I am more like the Thomas that, once he was shown, entered the field of service without ever again doubting or looking back. For this I am more indebted to Fools Crow than I am to anyone else. Thanks to him, I truly, as the Native American traditionalists of yesterday and today do, "believe in order to see," rather than "see in order to believe." The latter way is best only if there really is no God, and I am convinced that there is one. The famous theologian, Karl Barth, summed up the truth in a single encounter. When a professor friend told him that even after much research he just could not believe in God, the theologian responded, "Tell me what god you don't believe in, and I'm sure we will find that I do not believe in that god either." The point is clear. The god that people reject is not the true god, it is a god they have conjured up apart from proper education and understanding. In such cases, the least Fools Crow will do is to call their assumptions into question, and force them to reevaluate their position. Once they do, it is probable that they too will become little hollow bones through which supernatural power will flow out to the world.

It should be remembered that Fools Crow prepared himself between curings by regularly using the different concentration tools that *Wakan-Tanka* and the Helpers had given him for this purpose — the Purifications Lodge, the Yuwipi, his pipe, the three uncommon mental tools, visioning, the hoop, his drum and rattle, his distinctive curing and healing rites, and his smudging items. He never once relaxed about this, or took his relationship with the Higher Powers for granted. He knew that when power was abused, misused, or allowed to lay dormant, the holy or medicine person could lose it, or better said, that *Wakan-Tanka* and the Helpers would withdraw it. Once lost, it would remain so unless the medicine person involved changed his way of living for a long enough time to allow the Higher Powers to see that the change was sincere. Then if the medicine person petitioned passionately enough for a restored status, it might be considered.

Lest anyone think that, because of my reluctance to give the specific name for Fools Crow's medicine plants, I have negative thoughts about their use, let me clarify my position. I believe firmly in the value of plants for curing. Health care people the world over support this, and are bemoaning the rapid loss of plants as deforestation proceeds in virtually every country. It is already recognized that the plants offer curing agents that can have potent effect upon major illnesses. Africa can serve as a good example. I mentioned my acquaintance with Zulu chief Zubi Credo, who, by the way, is a graduate of Oxford. The bundle of plant roots he mailed me is astonishing. Only a short while ago, what the medicine people were doing with herbal remedies was classified as witchcraft. Now, scientists and physicians in increasing numbers are viewing their work as a valuable complement to modern medicine. Kurt Hostettman, a pharmacology professor at Lausanne University in Switzerland, says that if just ten percent of what healers tell us is true and can be proved scientifically, life could be much better for everyone. During a visit to East Africa he estimated that the continent had 200,000 plants not yet examined for their medical properties, plants that hold tremendous hope for the people in Africa and for Western people. In a two-year-old program similar to those in several other African countries, the Kenya Medical Research Institute has been sending its staff into the bush to interview medicine men. Back at the institute's laboratories in Nairobi, re-searchers try to identify the active ingredients of various leaves, roots, and tree bark used in folk medicine. The program is part of a global campaign, coordinated by the World Health Organization, to make greater use of traditional medicine, which in many areas offers a low-cost form of health care that is readily accepted by residents wary of modern medicine.[64] With this information in mind, Fools Crow's use of plants for curing has all of the support it needs as acceptable medical practice.

---

[64] As reported by The Associated Press, Monday, December 22, 1986.

12 FREEDOM FROM FEAR

"YOU HAVE TOLD ME THERE IS A DIFFERENCE BETWEEN CURING and healing," I said to Fools Crow, "and you have shown me what curing is and how you do it. What about healing, do you want to tell readers about that?"

"Yes," he said enthusiastically, and made an affirmative gesture with his hand.

"Before we talk about it," I said, "how do you know when a person who comes to you can not be cured or healed?"

"Looking into them and laying my hand on their shoulder tells me how big their faith is. If it isn't big enough, I don't undertake the cure or the healing."

"Can a person go away for awhile, pray about it, and then come back with enough faith?"

"That has happened many times."

"Do you sometimes do healing for those who aren't going to die, but who need a healthier and deeper relationship with *Wakan-Tanka?*"

"I have healed hundreds of people for this."

"Aren't there times when, even though their faith is big enough, a person cannot be cured?"

"Yes, and that is when I ask them if they would like to be healed."

"What do you do to learn how ill people are?"

"When I am wrapped up, *Wakan-Tanka* tells me. I see on my mind-screen the full dimensions of the person's illness. For example, I see that it has damaged their body beyond repair. All that can be cured in and through me is damage that can still be fixed. If an organ is nearly gone, or is entirely dead, nothing can be done. You can fix a hole in a rattle, but if it is smashed there is not much you can do. You sent to me a white man who had cancer. When I wrapped up I saw that his body was filled with it. It was terrible. Then I had to tell him that he was going to die, and asked him if he wanted to be healed. He asked me what healing was, and I told him that it was reaching peace, which was freedom from fear. You see, he needed to know that death was not an enemy, and that dying was only a quick step into the life we are all born for, into the place where we are secure with *Wakan-Tanka* forever. He was a young man, too young, he thought, to be dying. He was angry, and he blamed *Wakan-Tanka* for this. He did not think it was fair. Healing is what takes care of all of that. It gets rid of the anger and the hurt, and it also takes away the pain, both physically and mentally. When we are finished with the healing, the person is calm and ready, even anxious, to die. [This was certainly the case with the person he is referring to.] 'Die' is not really the best word, because it suggests that it is the end, when it is really the beginning. That is why, when I learned that Jesus told his followers that they just went to sleep, I liked his choice of words. They more truly say what I have been taught by *Wakan-Tanka*. We just go to sleep, and then wake up in His and *Tunkashila's* arms. I look forward to it."

"And how does the healing treatment go?"

"I ask the person to stay with me for four days, and I send his relatives home so we can be alone. If they are white people, I send them to the closest motel. If the weather is good, I fix a bed for the sick person outdoors under the trees. People are safe on my property. No one will bother them here. They eat the same food that I eat, and since it is usually not as good as what they normally eat, their training in humility begins with it. During the daytime they can smell the fresh air and the scent of the fields. One of the wonderful things about living here on the reservation is that nothing is tall enough to get between us and the Higher Powers. So we are more conscious of them than people who live in cities are. I tell the person to walk about and work on feeling close to Grandmother Earth and her creatures. We go on a hill and feel the winds come from the Directions, and we talk about what we hear in their sounds. I point out to them the colors of the earth and sky, and of the plants, and we do some becoming with interesting stones that we find. I explain to the person that all of these things have always been and will always be, and that this will be true for them too. If they are strong enough to stand it, we go into the Purifications Lodge. I take them out to pray with me, and I tell them some of the secrets I have told you. At night they lay on their bed under the stars, and I sit beside them for awhile. As we continue to talk, I tell them to think about *Wakan-Tanka* being up there and waiting to receive them. If they are Christians, I talk about Jesus' saying he went to make a place for them, and tell them that it is he who is waiting, because *Wakan-Tanka*, Grandfather, and Jesus are one and the same. If they are Jews I use the term God. I have also had people from Japan and India come to me, and I ask them what their name for *Wakan-Tanka* is, then I use it."

"What else do you do?"

"I treat them four times a day for four days, just as I do when I cure."

"But since they are going to die, do you use medicines."

"Yes," he answered with a smile, "but the medicines in this instance are medicines of the mind. We begin by using the two black cloth hoods that I have already told you about. We go into the house and sit in a darkened room. First I smoke (purify) us both, and then we sit on two chairs facing one another and around which I put down four pieces of colored cloth to mark the Four Directions. I put sage down too, and this makes an altar. We put the hoods on. The chairs are close together, and we hold hands some of the time but not all of the time. Sometimes I need my hands to fan the person with my eagle feather. What I do then is move the person's mind into my mind. I do this by singing my curing and healing song, and then telling them

to concentrate on moving into me. I make four moves with the feather
to pull it in. The person must continue to concentrate on this until
they see their spirits actually getting up from their body and moving
into me. I talk to them about spirit-movement, and I ask the Helpers,
all of them, to come and make this happen. There is a feeling of
expectancy in the room, and both of us are stirred up by it. Sometimes
we will see the pieces of colored cloth dancing around. We will both
see this. Afterwards the person will tell me he saw them move and
ask if I did. To confirm that I did, he will have me describe what I

saw, and it always matches the person's picture. Sometimes, we will see colors on our mind-screens — what white people call 'color auras.' The colors are different for different people, and each one is associated with a Direction. Then we know which Person we need to think the most about, and which powers will be the most useful to us in this particular case.

"When they are securely inside of my mind, we remove the hoods and I talk to them about getting rid of their pain and anger so that they can listen to *Wakan-Tanka* and the Helpers. An angry person can not and will not listen until they get rid of these blocks. We discuss this matter of resentment until the person begins to relax about it and to let it go. When I know this has happened and I am ready to congratulate them, we hold hands. I want them to feel through me not only my own love for them, but also *Wakan-Tanka's*. This is when the person begins to realize that *Wakan-Tanka* is not taking them away, that death is just the result of what happens in the world. What we do here with the black hoods is set the stage for the rest of what we will do. I always say 'we,' when I am talking to them, because I want to make certain the person knows we are doing the healing together, that it is not just I who will work out the healing. That makes them feel good about themselves, and their spirit rises. It begins to stand up.

"The next thing we do is use the sacred hoop. I described this hoop when we talked about curing, and we use it the same way in healing. If we need to make one, I show the person how to do it. A Sioux person might already have one, but these days they might not. The old ways are too far gone. Anyway, the hoop is the main medicine we use for the individual treatments during the four days. As you have seen, I make an altar on the ground with a piece of red cloth that is about twenty inches square, and I mark the corners as usual with the colored cloths. Then I lay the hoop on top of the cloth, with the hoop's colors facing in their proper directions. I put down a twist of sweetgrass on the east side of the cloth. It greets Sun each morning and asks him to send warmth from *Wakan-Tanka*. The sick person really needs this. As I have said, for healing all four colors are used. This is the big one, not like the regular problems where we use the small hoop to determine which of the Persons to call in. Then we walk mentally around the hoop together, and we talk about the Persons and their powers in the Directions as we walk. I do not do all of the talking. It is a shared discussion, and I encourage the person to say what is in their heart. One time we discuss what we feel, and I tell them what the Higher Powers led me to say when I communed with Them about the person. The next time we do more listening and see what we can learn. Sometimes we just pray silently together as we move around the hoop. If the person is a Lakota, we will sing sound songs together. Sometimes we will use the drum and the rattle. The whole idea continues to be one of reaching freedom from fear. Mainly, we start at the south by thinking about birth and rebirth. This time though, it is rebirth into the place where *Wakan-Tanka* dwells. Then we move to the west and think about renewal, but it is a renewal of attitude that we talk about, and not a renewal of body. When we get to the north we think about fertility, but it is fertility in the sense of having continual good thoughts and of leaving good things behind to help those who will mourn us. I remind them that the more people cry at a funeral the better, because we do not cry over things that are not important to us. We talk frankly about death, and we do not try to hide our feelings. When we get to the east, we think about thanksgiving and about being grateful for what we have been given. I point out to them that it is the quality of life that matters, and not the quantity. I tell them about people I knew who died young but had a better life and contributed more to others than some who died when they were old. I have the person review their life and think about the good things. We also talk about the bad, and how the best lessons of life are learned from it.

"Between treatments, I have the person walk around out in the fields and along the creek while they think about what we are doing together. If they are Indians they will have brought their pipe, and I ask them to pray with it. I show them how to do 'becoming,' and tell them to do this with rocks and twigs, plants and water. I have them hold a handful of earth, and make it come alive as they relate themselves to Grandmother Earth and the seasons. I point out that the seasons have followed a regular course since the beginning, and particularly how every winter is followed by a spring. As this happens with the seasons, I say, it also happens in life. Those who give themselves to *Wakan-Tanka* discover that every winter of life is followed by spring. So too, I tell them, their winter of illness will be followed by a spring that is more beautiful than anything they can imagine. I talk with them about what the place must be like where *Wakan-Tanka* and *Tunkashila* live. I do not see it like what the Bible says, but like the earth was in ancient times.

"Sometimes I warm my crystal in the sun or over a fire and have the person press it to their forehead to receive from the Higher Powers knowledge and understanding about life and death. If time permits, on the second or third day I help the person make a self-offering stick. But no two healings go exactly the same, and I make adjustments. Sometimes I am forced to leave out certain parts.

"Another thing I have the person make is a string of 405 tobacco offerings to lay down beside our altars. This takes a lot of time, but it is all part of helping them to sink deeper and deeper into what we are doing, and into their relationship with *Wakan-Tanka*. I make sure the person knows how the 405 White Stone Men do their work. The amount of time we take for everything is good, because it shuts out everything that will hurt or interfere with what we are doing. We move slowly, and we do not hurry with anything. Unlike the curing ceremonies, I do not keep raising the pace or aim toward a climax. There is no climax to be reached here. Instead it is a return to peace.

"Between treatments, if the person feels well enough, we make music and sing. This is done softly. Now and then the person will even get up and dance. When they do this they are lost in their thoughts, and I do not intrude. I just keep playing my drum, and I sing sound songs. There were times in the past when I was able to bring in some singers and musicians. Once I had a flute player who would come when I invited him, and he made a beautiful contribution. Often, the person and I would cry while the flute musician was playing . . . not much, just a little, and our tears were tears of joy over knowing the great secrets of death that we were sharing. During these last years, singers and musicians who do things the ancient way are getting harder to find. There are still some, but they do not live close by. I hope they will be at my funeral."

(From what I have heard about Fools Crow's funeral, and this includes a tape I was sent by Richard Carey, the singers and musicians he referred to were there to honor him and consign him to sleep. If they read this, they will be pleased to know what was in his heart as he talked about them.)

"Do you ever do the hollow bones cleansing and filling ritual with the person, or does that matter at this time?"

"Only if it appears that they have some time to live. But I have the person do lots of deep breathing to relax."

"Is there anything else I should know about?"

"Yes, before the person goes home, I tell them to continue doing all of the things I have taught them. *Wakan-Tanka* often gives me information about a strange and unexpected thing that the person will see and do just before they die. I tell the person and his family all about this. It will be something that confirms the fact that the person has reached peace and is ready to go to sleep, and also something that tells them when the person is safely with *Wakan-Tanka*. In the case of that young person you sent me who had cancer, I was shown that just before he died, even though he was not able to speak Lakota, he would sing a song in perfect Lakota, and that in the evening after he went to his sleep, the stars and other heavenly bodies would move to form a certain pattern. His family would see this happen. I made a drawing in the dirt to show them what the pattern would be like. These things are exactly what happened, and death for that person turned out to be a happy time instead of what it would have been had he not come here to be healed."

"In my personal experiences," I said, "I have learned that when freedom from fear has come to a dying person, they sometimes live much longer than is expected. Is this the way it is with people who come to you?"

"Most of the time," he replied.

"What about the family? You said that you send them away while you are treating the patient, but do you take some time to talk with them and help their understanding?"

"Sometimes," he said, "but one of the last things I tell the person to do is to ask their family to sit with them while they tell them about some of the things that have gone on while they were with me. This helps the person review and relive what we have done and sharpens his thinking about it. It never fails that after the person has moved on to be with *Wakan-Tanka*, the family will write to me or come to me to tell me how grateful they are and what the strange things were that happened at the moment of going to sleep. One of my relatives reads the letters to me so that I can know all of this."

As I conclude this chapter, the newspapers are reporting that University of Chicago archaeologists and anthropologists are heralding the discovery of a huge, four thousand-year-old Babylonian temple in southern Iraq that "may shed new light on the origins of medicine."[65]

The temple is located in the ancient desert city of Nippur, which is generally considered to be the cradle of human civilization about eight thousand years ago. "This temple could tell us more about ancient medicine than we've ever known before," the discoverers say, "and its prominence may mean that concerns about health and medicine played a bigger role in the people's everyday lives than previously had been suspected."

The temple is believed to honor the goddess of healing, Gula, to whom sick people would come bearing treasures in hopes of being cured. Current knowledge of ancient medicine, the article continues, is based largely on herbal treatments prescribed in early clay medical tests. Mesopotamians had a highly developed system of health care that included physicians trained to cure illness, magicians who worked spells to ward off evil spirits, and priests who prayed for healing when physicians and magicians were unsuccessful. For internal maladies, people would drink potions made of various herbs mixed in beer, milk, water, wine, or, occasionally, cow's urine. Other common practices involved enemas made from wool soaked in liquids, suppositories, and a feather to tickle the back of one's throat to induce vomiting. For rashes, skin cancer, and other external problems, they would apply herbs to the affected area. "Only the privileged had access to educated physicians. . . . Most people had recourse only to the herbal doctor who learned his trade by observing others."

---

[65] *The Orange County Register*, June 21, 1990.

What impresses me about this discovery is not the temple itself or what it portends. It is the fact that, in Fools Crow, who carried on so much of the heritage of his people, we already have everything the archaeologists want to know about ancient medicine. What the Babylonians did, the Native Americans did, and apparently did it better. If the professionals looked at the Native Americans more carefully, they would see that this is so. In Fools Crow alone, we find extensive and engrossing answers to both physical and mental curing and healing. He was physician and psychiatrist combined. Holistic health in its finest form has been at our very doorstep here in America. Why go so far afield to discover what, after all the digging has been done, will for the most part remain speculation?

13 A BIG LIFT

SEEMINGLY NAIVE CONCEPTS . . . PRIMITIVE THOUGHTS, IF YOU will . . . a child's understanding perhaps . . . can often reveal things that the scientific and illuminated mind will seldom see.

For example, while the Native Americans adamantly and uniformly deny that the highest Native American god was the sun, non-Indian observers have often claimed that the Indians were sun worshipers.[66] Fools Crow readily admitted that Native Americans have recognized the beneficial and powerful attributes of the sun, who to them was a Person. And so they reverenced it as a holy being. "Can life exist and continue without it?" the Sioux would ask themselves as they experienced the rigors of midwestern winters. But there was another, and perhaps more important reason why they reverenced the sun . . . their view of *Wakan-Tanka*. As He traveled about to watch over his magnificent creation, He often stayed for a time in the sun, where the warmth of His being infused it. Therefore, the warmth we feel here on earth is in truth the warmth of *Wakan-Tanka's* person.

---

[66] *Fools Crow*, 1979, p. 119.

The warmer the day is, the more aware the Native Americans are of Him and His closeness.

One should measure this awareness against scientific truths in terms of what it means to people who are hurting, and then decide which of the views does the most for humanity. When people are ill or hurting from any kind of pain, which concept will give them strength and hope, and which will bring more happiness? Knowing that God made it possible for people to feel His closeness was essential to the well-being of the Native Americans, and that is one of the reasons why most of their major rituals have been held in mid-summer.

I have been with Pueblo, Apache, and Cherokee medicine men and know that after smudging their ritual items with smoke, they either warm them in the sun or over a fire prior to their use in ceremonies. This has been a standard practice among all Native American tribes. Those who are acquainted with the altars used by the Pueblo Indians know they have carved and painted symbols on them that represent the Higher Powers' presence to "overlook and assist" the ritual proceedings in the kiva. This acknowledgement of supernatural presence heightens the clan member's awareness that they are being closely guided, and therefore are assured a successful outcome. They do not do what they do alone, or even at a distance from God.

Fools Crow recognized these same things, and he was also taught that the Higher Powers have blessed the world in a special way through fire. "From the beginning of time," he said, "our people have known that the fires we make are a little piece of Sun, and as such they bring the warmth of *Wakan-Tanka's* presence down to the very surface of earth itself. Volcanoes are reminders of this truth, and of how much power there truly is in fire. Fire is hidden in everything, because everything will burn. Wherever fire is, *Wakan-Tanka* is, which is why fire is part of all of our rituals, and when the smoke rises up from it we put into the smoke — like a letter into an envelope — our prayers of thanksgiving to be carried up to *Wakan-Tanka* and His Helpers."

"Do you really believe that volcanoes were put here on earth to remind us of the power of fire?"

"If we believe they are, they are. Does it matter whether or not a scientist thinks this? People respond to what they believe and live accordingly. The beliefs do for us what needs to be done in our relationship with *Wakan-Tanka*. What does the scientist's belief do for him so far as *Wakan-Tanka* is concerned?"

"If *Wakan-Tanka's* presence is in the fire," I said, "why do you need to send prayers up to Him?"

"I am sitting here," he answered. "I am present. But my body also gives off heat, and if I come close to you, you will feel this heat. What you feel is me, and it is part of my presence. It is like this with *Wakan-Tanka*. His body gives off heat just as ours does, only it is a much greater kind of heat. There is great power in it. Sun and fire are ways of letting us feel this and get strength and hope from it without being burned up. It is like that burning bush that Moses saw in the desert."

He had me smiling to myself over the way he had picked up the Bible stories the priests had told him and applied them to his own understandings about spiritual things. I nodded my head several times before continuing. "Then *Wakan-Tanka* makes himself known in two ways: through His actual presence and through the experience of His presence?"

"Yes. But He is never actually present in the sense that His total person has come to be with us. This is just a power that He sends to make us know that He is with us."

"Are Sun and fire as close as the warmth of His person can come to us?"

"No. In the crystal it comes right up to us and touches us. Crystals are very special among stones. They have been given an unusual power. Their clarity [translucence] makes it possible for *Wakan-Tanka* and His Helpers to send messages that pass through them to us. They are like the wires that carry electricity and telephone talk."

"Why," I said, "do you think *Wakan-Tanka* needs a crystal? You have told me that he sometimes speaks directly to you."

Fools Crow answered without the slightest hesitation. "He doesn't need crystals, we do. The tools He gives us are part of our deeper immersion into communion with Him. The crystals are given

to us for our sakes, not His. It is we who need both the time and the tools required to concentrate our minds, hearts and bodies as we commune with *Wakan-Tanka* and the Helpers."

"I have noticed," I said, "that you always warm your crystal in the sun, or over a fire or a candle, before you use it for any purpose."

"This is to pick up the warmth of *Wakan-Tanka* and the Helpers and bring them closer than even the fire can. The crystal can bring Them right up to the person who needs to be enlightened, cured, or healed. You have seen that I use the crystal to look into a person to find causes and to reflect curing or healing power into a patient. When

I do this, I also place the crystal right on the skin of the person. They receive strength, encouragement and hope from this."

I had indeed been privileged to watch Fools Crow as he employed his crystal for illumination, curing and healing. For illumination, he pressed it against the patient's forehead, or against his own if he wanted personal help. The information received, he explained, passed through the crystal and into his mind. What he actually did for curing was to hold the warmed crystal sideways between the forefingers and thumbs of his two hands as he waved it above the patient's body to reflect sunlight into the patient. Then he pressed the crystal lightly against the patient's torso at different places in a stamping kind of motion — on the front, back and sides. While he did this, Fools Crow was always singing his stone song, and he now and then looked upward toward the Higher Power's dwelling place. Usually the patient would cry out in pain when Fools Crow touched a tender spot. Sometimes a certain area would be reached where the crystal would emit a soft glow, whose color varied according to the problem. If neither of these things happened, he would stop now and then as he moved the crystal and bend forward to look through it into the patient's body. All of this was part of searching for the illness and its cause. Sooner or later Fools Crow would discover what these were. Then he would wrap up to learn how to treat them.

The only crystal Fools Crow used, and even it was used sparingly, was a plain quartz crystal that was medium-sized and not especially pretty. He did not use colored stones as many of the New Age people do. On one occasion when a friend of mine brought him a dazzling array of colored crystals in a magnificent wooden box, Fools Crow stared at them as though he couldn't imagine why anyone would bother to assemble such a collection. My friend was greatly dismayed, and shortly after that found a buyer for the stones.

I asked Fools Crow where he obtained his crystal, and he responded that Stirrup had given it to him and taught him how to use it.

"Did Stirrup have you stay with him while he cured and healed patients?" I asked.

"Many times. It was part of my training. At first, I spent one whole week with him, and after that he asked me to come and watch while he treated people."

"Was Stirrup a holy man or a medicine man?"

"He was a holy man, and the best kind of teacher. He loved everyone, just as I do, and his students and patients always responded to this."

"Stirrup had other pupils besides yourself?"

"Before me and after me."

"Was Stirrup also a warrior?"

"There were times when he was forced to stand with our people, just as Black Elk was. Except for the Custer battle, we were usually outnumbered, and all of the men had to fight. But Stirrup told me he did not like fighting because it was only a temporary answer for anything, and made a real peace even harder to obtain."

I returned to the subject of Sun, fire, and crystals, and asked Fools Crow what all three together meant to him. He had to think about that for awhile, and he and Dallas launched into one of the long conversations in Lakota that were so vexing to me because I could understand very little of them. Now and then during the discussions, Dallas would turn to me with a cheerful smile and tell me a little about what Fools Crow was saying. Then he would solicit my response. He relayed that to Fools Crow, and the conversation continued. Finally in this instance Dallas summed it up with a response that was like those single Chinese characters that can say volumes of things.

"Closeness," Dallas said, "he says closeness."

"That's all you have after twenty minutes of talking!" I exclaimed.

Dallas was pleased with himself and grinned broadly. He was always delighted when he could sum things up so neatly. "OK," he said, "Fools Crow says that Sun, fire, and crystals are *Wakan-Tanka's* way of coming closer and closer to us, and even touching us. This allows us to experience Him in a wonderful way, and we are given a big lift by it."

"Fools Crow said that, big lift?"

"Those are my words," Dallas replied with a triumphant toss of his head. "I think that says it."

I had grown to love Dallas. He was a magnificent person and an exceptional friend. I let him have his way. Remembering this, I have made his summary the title for this chapter.

Fools Crow felt left out, and held up his hand to interrupt us. "Tell people, in your book, to remember and to think about the closeness of *Wakan-Tanka*. If they live in this wisdom it will give them endless strength and hope."

14 RELUCTANT GOOD-BYES

IN HIS EULOGY PRESENTED AT FOOLS CROW'S FUNERAL, AMERican Indian Movement leader Russell Means gave Fools Crow credit for returning to the Sioux the sacred rite of Spirit Keeping. No doubt this is true, but Fools Crow did not tell me that he deserved credit for bringing it back. Alice C. Fletcher describes this profound rite in "The Shadow or Ghost Lodge."[67] Frances Densmore's informants also recount what she calls the "Ceremony of the Spirit."[68] Joseph Epes Brown gives Black Elk's extensive treatment of the origin of the rite under the titles, "The Keeping of the Soul," and "The Release of the Soul."[69] Under the title, "Spirit Keeping," I report it in my *Sundancing* and *Secret Pathways* books.

---

[67] Fletcher, 1884, Nos. 3, 4, and calls it, "The Keeping of the Soul."
[68] Densmore, 1918, pp. 77-84.
[69] Brown, 1953, pp. 10-30.

Spirit Keeping is a Sioux pathway that centers itself in the beautiful thoughts and love inspired in the people involved. In ancient times it was widely practiced. But early missionaries considered the ritual to be heathen and, as they so commonly did with other Native American rites, sought to eliminate the practice. In 1890, a law was passed forbidding its performance. Today it is rarely held, but I had the privilege of seeing part of it enacted at a Sun Dance at Rosebud on July 3, 1975. In this instance, a young woman who had been given a special healing ceremony in 1974 had died shortly before the 1975 Sun Dance was held. Since she had promised that she would participate in the dance if she was alive in July of 1975, a close female friend held a Spirit Keeping Ceremony at the dance to keep her vow.

Spirit Keeping is one of the seven rituals given to the Sioux by White Buffalo Maiden, who brought the Sacred Pipe. It is performed for a deceased loved one, usually a child or youth, and it serves a double purpose: comforting broken hearts by keeping at earth level the spirit, or soul, of the dead person for a specified period of time; and promoting good thoughts, love, and unity throughout the Sioux nation.

The Spirit Keeper's role demands considerable sacrifice. Those who agree to accept it must be of good repute and willing to separate themselves from worldly concerns and involvements for as long as the ceremony lasts, which may be a year. During this period, the Keeper concentrates intently upon the central purpose of the ritual, which is to prolong through constant prayer the mourning period. Spirit Keeping makes the parting more bearable for family and friends. After the traditional purification rites have been conducted in the Purifications Lodge, a lock of the deceased's hair and several other small possessions that had been theirs are fashioned into an exotic spirit bundle and put in a place of honor in the Keeper's lodge. A Spirit Post is carved from cottonwood, painted with a face that represents the deceased, and placed upright in the ground at the entrance to the Keeper's lodge for the duration of the rite. In the releasing ceremony, the bundle and the post are held up to Sun while prayers are said, then the spirit is sent off with further prayers to *Wakan-Tanka*.

Frank and I did not talk overly much about his views regarding what happens after death, although it has been seen that in his healing rites he discussed death with his patients, and also the matter of preparing for it. He was comfortable with the belief that the faithful go directly to be with *Wakan-Tanka*. He did not fear death, and he was not persuaded by Roman Catholic teachings about Purgatory and Hell (in fairness I note here that Roman Catholic priests in the United States do not seem to be talking much about Purgatory either). Fools Crow subscribed to the idea that human beings create most of their own problems here on earth by failing to entrust themselves to *Wakan-Tanka* and the Helpers. During one conversation, he flatly denied there was any such thing as reincarnation. "We are born on this earth," he said, "and we die here, and then we go to be forever with *Wakan-Tanka.*" If he harbored any ideas about family reunions in heaven, or of the Sioux being in some great encampment as Black Elk did, he did not say so. I am guessing, of course, that he believed being with *Wakan-Tanka* for all eternity is what all of us should cherish more than anything else, and I think he would say that once we are fully with *Wakan-Tanka* and *Tunkashila* we will not possibly want for anything more — including a continuance of life as it is lived here on earth.

During one conversation about healing, I asked him whether he thought the races would remain their same colors once they went to be with *Wakan-Tanka*.

"No," he said, and then began to smile the little smile he used when he was about to make a joke, "we will all be one color."

Out of the corner of my eye I could see Dallas coming alert and getting ready to share in whatever Fools Crow was about to say. "Which will be . . . ?" I asked tentatively, thinking I knew that his answer would be red.

"Orange!" he exclaimed and whooped explosively. When he and Dallas finally calmed down, Fools Crow added, "It has to be some color that none of us are now."

I did tell Fools Crow about the Pueblo and Cherokee ways of calling back the dead, and asked him whether the Sioux did this. His answer was that while he believed calling back was possible, he was not personally taught to do it, and he did not know any Sioux medicine man who did. He recalled that, during the Ghost Dances of 1890, the entranced Sioux, wearing their painted ghost shirts, saw their ancestors coming back to life together with the buffalo herds, but that was all he knew of, and he ended by saying that for the Sioux and other Indians nothing but tragic problems resulted from the dance.

"Soul" or "Spirit" Keeping — whichever one prefers to call it — has been something uniquely important to the Sioux people, and I urge everyone to read the materials I have cited regarding it. It is heartwarming to think of people loving their own so much they cannot bear to part with them until they must. If I had known earlier about Fools Crow's role in its restoration, you can be certain that I would have attempted to learn more about it from the old holy man. In particular, I would like to have asked him was why he believed that the rite deserved to be restored and ought to be continued. Based upon the time I spent with him over a period of several years, and the close relationship we had, my guess is that his answer would be something like . . . "Spirit Keeping is the expression of true love." He would go on to say that, "It is a way to show personal love in such a fashion that no one can mistake its depth and sincerity. The Spirit Keeping rite is a way of stating, in poetic form, that our years together have been so gratifying that I cannot bear to let you go. Even though I know it must happen, give me some time to adjust to the idea. Perhaps in six months or a year I will be ready to accept it."

If my speculation accurately represents Fools Crow's view, the Spirit Keeping rite flies directly into the face of the depiction of Native Americans of the past as being backward and savage. Instead, Spirit Keeping requires us to take a closer look at their ancient lifeway, where once we do we will see a dimension of it hitherto missed or ignored — a tenderness and a concern that ought to underscore our own relationships with one another. The least it will do is raise up a mirror in which we can see an honest reflection of ourselves: Do we live in bonds of perfect unity? Which do we seek in human relationships? Is it the highest place? Is it equality? Or, is it putting others first?

All we need do to get the full thrust of Spirit Keeping is to accept the challenge to make our own spirit post for someone we say we love. Then we can ask ourselves some questions about it. What will the post itself be like? With what care will it be made? What will we attach to it to express our feelings? What will we sacrifice to watch over it and to nourish it? How far will we go to show the depth of our love? And, when the year of watching is done, will we make the release of the person's soul a fitting tribute to the love we shared?

What, in substance, is Spirit Keeping? It is the Sioux way of saying a reluctant good-bye. It is the kind of good-bye I have for my friend Fools Crow. He certainly deserves a splendid Spirit Post and bundle. Were it not that such things aren't done for the elderly who have had a full life and are now secure in *Wakan-Tanka*, I would be making one for him. I have enough of his personal things to do that, including a wonderful group photograph he gave me of Fannie, their first two children, his father Eagle Bear, and himself. Now that I think about it, perhaps Fools Crow has "wittingly" joined with me in fashioning his own spirit post and bundle in the *Fools Crow* and *Fools Crow: Wisdom and Power* books. Certainly they are a way of keeping the Old Lord of the Holy Men close at hand — not for just a year, but always.

15 THE END AND THE BEGINNING

MORE THAN A YEAR BEFORE HE DIED, A REPORT WAS WIDELY circulated that Fools Crow was dead. People began calling to tell me this, but when I checked to verify it, I discovered that he was still alive. For awhile though, he probably wished the rumor was true. What had actually happened was that some unknown person or persons had broken into his house while he was away and taken everything he owned except a camp cot and the clothes he was wearing. The last of his costumes, food, bedding, clothing and furniture was gone, and the old Lord of the Holy Men was left desolate. His relatives moved him into a run-down trailer on his daughter's property that had no utilities and no well. It was here that Dik Darnell, pursuing the same rumor I was, found Fools Crow. He was sitting on the camp cot, alone and uncharacteristically despondent. Several of us pitched in to get him a well and the other things he needed, so that he was able to finish his life in some comfort.

Mutual friends like Buddy Red Bow who visited him after the robbery reported to me that he told them, "The wagon is coming for me," meaning that he knew death was near. He had, in fact, willed this to be so for several years and told me that more than once. Many who heard about the robbery are unable to understand how it could happen to such a grand, respected, and loving person as Fools Crow. They simply do not know how abysmal life has become for most of the residents at Pine Ridge, Rosebud, and some other reservations. Crimes of every kind are common today, and the criminals are no respecters of persons. Usually, the lawlessness is spawned by drinking and poverty, and the fact that it happened to Fools Crow by no means depreciates the general respect in which he was held. His funeral and burial services are eloquent testimony to this truth.

Unfortunately, however, those who committed the robbery were not alone in their shabby treatment of the grand old man. When a certain museum and gallery opened in the Black Hills in 1989, Fools Crow, as the eminent representative of the Sioux, was among those invited to make a speech. I was among the artists who were invited to share in the first annual group show. Fortunately I declined, and I wish Fools Crow had too. Native Americans who were present told me that the way he was treated was shameful. They put this sensitive and loving ninety-eight-year-old man on stage in P.T. Barnum fashion and in borrowed costume. It was for only a few minutes. They gave him no opportunity to say anything of consequence, ushered him unceremoniously offstage, and afterward ignored him completely. I'm glad I wasn't there to witness it and to react as I know I would have. The wagon is loaded with mystifying bedfellows.

I was being treated for an eye problem by an ophthalmologist and could not attend the funeral rites for Fools Crow, but several friends were kind enough to fill me in on how they went.[70]

According to what I was told, death came quietly to Fools Crow in the home of his grandchildren sometime during the night of Monday, November 27, 1989. Outside, a blizzard raged. If he heard it, he probably smiled to himself as he remembered how many times he had fought and beaten the irascible Cold Maker. Born in June of 1890, if he had lived another seven months he would have reached the

---

[70] I am principally indebted to Richard Carey for the funeral information.

venerable age of one hundred, which is fifty-eight more years than the life-expectancy of Native Americans living on the Pine Ridge and Rosebud reservations today. How did he achieve this? The answer is clear. It was due to the glorious kind of spiritual life he had led, and surely with *Wakan-Tanka's* blessing, for the Higher Powers have never had a more faithful servant.

The first call came from Dik at 8 a.m., California time. "Grandpa is gone," he said. We visited for only a few minutes, sharing our agreement that we were glad it was over, that the wagon had finally arrived. Several other calls came that day and the next, including one from Buddy. I explained to each caller that because of the eye problem I could not join them for the funeral, but I don't think it would have mattered to Frank. We had said our reluctant good-byes long before. There was also something I would not have wanted to see — Fools Crow being laid to rest in a blue polyester suit instead of his buckskin ceremonial costume, and without any of his medicine items to attend him in the spirit world.

I do not, of course, blame any of the people of Pine Ridge for this. They did the best they could under the circumstances. What was gone, was gone, and could not be resurrected. Consolation is found in the splendid funeral they gave him.

Immediately after the storm, the weather turned incredibly beautiful. Yet I chose to think it was no accident that the blizzard had roared through to mark his passing. It was Cold Maker's final salute, and now Sun had returned as he does at winter solstices to chase Cold Maker away. By Monday, the skies were clear, and the temperature was so warm that people were comfortable in only a sweater.

A memorial service was held in the Little Wound School gymnasium in Kyle, where Fools Crow was laid on a buffalo robe in an open casket. At one end of the room was a large, white, empty tipi, and at both ends of the casket were tables and racks containing memorabilia and offerings that were to be distributed in a giveaway after burial. I doubt that any of this belonged to Fools Crow. More probably it was contributed by family and friends. Behind the casket was an extended ladder on which a blanket was hung, and perched above the blanket was a stuffed golden eagle with outstretched wings. A rope was stretched along the wall at head height, and a dozen or more star quilts were hung on it. The smell of burning sage permeated the air.

On Saturday night, Sunday, and Monday, between five hundred and seven hundred mourners, most of whom were Native Americans, were in attendance at any one time. Has there been a larger traditional funeral at Pine Ridge in recent times? I have no way of knowing, but I doubt it. (I've heard nothing about the service for Black Elk, and I suspect that his reputation grew dimensionally only when Neihardt presented him to the world in *Black Elk Speaks*. This superb book has sold consistently since the day it was published, and today Black Elk is better known than any other holy or medicine person.)

The funeral services were originally scheduled for the Episcopal Mediator Church, which sits high on a grassy hill outside Kyle. But it was far too small a structure to accommodate those who came, so the memorial service was shifted to the gymnasium. Mourners sat either on bleacher seats or on folding chairs that were set up on the gymnasium floor. People visited as mourners do, but the atmosphere was one of great reverence. Mourners who volunteered, both Native American and white, were permitted to take turns standing next to the casket as honor guards with feather staff in hand — so that Fools Crow was never unattended.

There was a shared communion of dried buffalo meat, and also boiled dog, which was served by a Yuwipi medicine man. Dog meat is a regular part of the traditional Yuwipi ceremony.

AIM leader Russell Means gave what Richard Carey describes as, "an impressive talk that deserved being recorded." He mentioned that the Spirit Keeping and Sun Dance ceremonies had been outlawed by the United States Government in 1890, and gave Fools Crow credit for bringing them back into the open.[71] Means also said Fools Crow felt that the youth of the Sioux reservations did not deserve to receive the knowledge they could have received had they lived as they should. He mentioned my book about Fools Crow, and that Grandpa had loved the people of AIM. Means also credited Fools

---

[71] My *Sundancing* and *Fools Crow* books gave information about Fools Crow's responsibility for the return of the Sun Dance for public purposes, and with piercing.

Crow with the peaceful ending of the Wounded Knee holdout. He closed by stating that "Grandfather Fools Crow" had left a legacy showing how beautiful the Native Americans have been as a race, and said that wherever there are Indians in schools they should be taught about Fools Crow.[72]

At Dik's suggestion, Richard called the White House to notify President Bush of Fools Crow's death. It is believed that Bush responded by sending a wire to the family of Fools Crow's daughter expressing his condolences.

As Fools Crow's casket was moved out of the gymnasium and onto a wooden wagon that would carry him to his burial site, drumming began. The wagon had a coup stick attached to its right side and it was drawn by a matched pair of brown horses with white markings on their noses. It was painted green, and had large orange wheels. The casket itself was draped with a multi-colored star quilt, and over this was laid crosswise a folded Pendleton blanket.

An ambulance led the funeral procession for the five-mile trip to the Episcopal cemetery, and the cortege stretched out for three and a half miles. Behind it was a pickup truck carrying drummers and singers who chanted traditional burial songs, using a slow parade beat, and women who trilled. After the truck came two men on horseback who carried staffs. They were followed by a white-and-brown spotted horse that bore no rider, but was draped with a star quilt that was trimmed with a band of red. A warbonnet with white feathers tipped in black sat upright on the quilt.

Sixty men on horseback rode double file behind the horse, followed by a limousine carrying family members and private cars carrying mourners.

The casket was lowered into the ground at approximately 2:35 p.m., and curiously, Fools Crow, a baptized Roman Catholic, was buried in the Episcopal cemetery in front of the grave of not Kate, his second wife, but of his first wife, Fannie, who had died in 1954. The specific reasons for this were not given to me, but I have my personal suspicions as to why it was done. One is that the choice

---

[72] Fools Crow's part in ending the holdout is fully described in *Fools Crow*, pp. 191-193.

plainly reveals Fools Crow's devotion to traditional life — that he never truly gave himself over to the Roman Catholic church, and that the priests at Pine Ridge knew this. Another reason might be that Fools Crow's father, Eagle Bear, was buried in this cemetery.

As the casket lay suspended on three tree trunks laid crosswise over the open pit, the final Lakota burial services were performed. A twelve-inch-deep hole was dug at the foot of the pit and filled with heated rocks. Sage was placed on the ground nearby to be sprinkled on the rocks. Several medicine men took turns placing handfuls of earth on the casket while they prayed in Lakota, and as they did this, water was poured on the rocks and sage-tinged steam and smoke rose into the air to carry Fools Crow's spirit and their prayers up to *Wakan-Tanka.*

A medicine man walked around the perimeter of the burial pit and purified it by fanning sage-smoke into it with an eagle feather. Bits of traditional foods, such as fry bread and fruit pudding, were dropped into the grave. Their spirits would accompany and nourish Fools Crow on his last journey to *Wakan-Tanka's* dwelling place. Just before the casket was lowered, Nellie and Matthew Two Bulls, teachers at Red Cloud Indian School in the town of Pine Ridge, sang an honoring song that was especially written for Fools Crow. In it, they refer to him as *Wanbli Mato,* Eagle Bear, which was his true Lakota name.

After lowering the casket into the pit, eight pallbearers who wore feathered warbonnets covered the casket with a multi-colored star quilt. Then, as four hundred weeping mourners watched, the pallbearers shoveled dirt into the pit. It was a beautifully done burial, with appropriate traditional touches — a burial which, if the Old Lord of the Holy Men could have watched it, would have made him proud. All that remains now is to provide his grave with a fitting headstone.

The mourners returned to the gymnasium, where a traditional feast and giveaway were held.

An extensive obituary published on November 28 in the *Rapid City Journal* states that Fools Crow had followed his vision quests, "which directed him into a life of healing and tribal leadership. He saw," it says, "alcoholism and jealousy as the greatest curses for the Indian people." The writer cites an interview carried in the *Journal* in its Centennial Edition in February of 1989. It reports that Fools Crow said he realized the world was changing, and that life was not like it used to be, but that modern problems must be dealt with "through cooperation and without losing sight of the old ways." Fools Crow is also quoted as saying, "We need peace and understanding and unity of young and old, Indians and non-Indians alike. We must all stand together for the reason of peace and tranquility of life for all." Fools Crow, it goes on, "believed respect, generosity, courage, knowledge, and wisdom were the keys to the survival of the Lakota culture. These values start from the home. They are taught there and carried into the world. You must first better understand yourself before you can express yourself to others. The Lakota values help you do this." In closing, the article mentions my *Fools Crow* book, and discloses that I describe in it what I call, "the noble legacy left by Fools Crow."

As friends have sent me copies of various eulogies written for Fools Crow, I have noticed that they concur in mentioning his profound love for all humankind — Native Americans and non-Native Americans alike.

In the *Fools Crow* book I say I would not be surprised if a "dramatic sound" accompanied his death. People who were not with him when he died, but were nearby, say they heard nothing. But they miss my real meaning, which is that in death he will be heard in a way and a dimension he could never have attained in life. This has always been the way of things. Jesus put it succinctly when he recalled that a prophet is without honor in his own home. He had to leave family and friends to accomplish things with those who didn't hinder him because they observed and remembered his human frailties. All of us become aware of this problem as during an argument we are called upon to listen to a review of our past mistakes and statements. "Saved things" are carefully designed to cut us down to size or as a way of keeping situations even. Fools Crow escaped this kind of censure better than most, but not entirely. There was always jealousy and there were political rivals. Now that he has departed no one has anything to gain by demeaning him. The story and teachings of Fools Crow will spread far beyond where they already have. Before long his name and insights will be known everywhere. He has left me with a whole new definition of what "civilized" means, and with a greatly enhanced portrait of God in communication with His creation.

The pipe Fools Crow passed on to me, and which he used for forty years after Iron Cloud passed it on to him, is on permanent display in the Center for Western Studies at Augustana College, in Sioux Falls, South Dakota. Visitors can see it there, and I trust that as they study it they will reflect for a few moments on the grand Old Lord of the Holy Men, whose physical end has come, but whose dauntlessness and quintessence goes forth in all of its fullness to carry on his service to *Wakan-Tanka* and the Helpers.

Will the Teton Sioux ever have another holy man like Fools Crow? There are a few men among them who might qualify — if they survive, and if they will live as he did. There are those who are connected with the "new theology," and interesting things are happening with the Native American Church. It will be engrossing to see what the future brings.

Have I, in writing this book, revealed everything Frank told me? Of course not. Neither of my two books about him tell the entire story of what he said and did while I was with him, and I know very little about what went on after that time. This book covers only his central and most important understandings and rituals. The exact way to do some rituals and some songs I will probably keep forever to myself. Other things I may share with some of those select people whom I have already met, or will meet down the road. I will know who the right ones are, because, as he taught me to do, I will look into them with my mind, touch them with my eyes, decide with my heart, and I will put my hand on their shoulder to see whether it becomes hot or cold.

Meanwhile, by keeping my promise to Frank and passing on to you this second kind of material, I place in your hands a sacred trust. As I do so, I repeat what he said — "Anyone who is willing to live the life I have led can do the things that I do." The opportunity to meet this challenge is entirely yours. You can soar as high as you would like to in spiritual service. Who knows, *Wakan-Tanka* may even now be calling you to holiness, and to be a little hollow bone.

BIBLIOGRAPHY

Brown, Joseph Epes, *The Sacred Pipe*, Norman, University of Oklahoma Press, 1953.

Carson, Rachel, *Silent Spring*, Houghton Mifflin Company, Boston, 1962.

Commoner, Barry, *Making Peace with the Planet*, Random House, Inc., New York, N.Y., 1975 and 1990.

Densmore, Frances, *Teton Sioux Music*, Smithsonian Institution, Bureau of American Ethnology, Bulletin 61, Washington, D.C., 1918.

Eiseley, Loren, *The Invisible Pyramid*, Charles Scribner's Sons, New York, N.Y., 1970.

Fletcher, Alice C., *The Shadow or Ghost Lodge*, Annual Report of the Peabody Museum, Nos. 3, 4, 1884.

Gribbin, John, *Hothouse Earth*, Grove Weidenfeld, New York, N.Y., 1990.

Katz, Richard, *Boiling Energy*, 1982, Harvard University Press, Cambridge, MA, London, England.

Mails, Thomas, *Fools Crow*, Doubleday & Company, Inc., Garden City, N.Y., 1979.

Mails, Thomas, *Pueblo Children of the Earth Mother*, Vols 1 & 2, Doubleday & Company, Inc., 1983.

Mails, Thomas, *Secret Native American Pathways — A Guide to Inner Peace*, Council Oak Books, Tulsa, OK, 1988.

Mails, Thomas, *Sundancing at Rosebud & Pine Ridge*, Center for Western Studies, Sioux Falls, S.D., 1978.

Neihardt, John G., *Black Elk Speaks*, William Morrow & Company, New York, N.Y., 1932, and University of Nebraska Press, Lincoln, 1979.

Schell, Johnathan,*The Fate of the Earth*, Alfred A. Knopf, Inc., New York, N.Y., 1982.

Waugh, Earle H., and Prithipaul, K. Dad, eds., *Native Religious Traditions, Joint International Symposium of Elders & Scholars*, Edmonton, Alta. published by the Canadian Corporation for Studies in Religion, 1977.

Other books by
Thomas E. Mails

Mystic Warriors of the Plains

Fools Crow

Pueblo Children of the Earth Mother, Vol. 1

Pueblo Children of the Earth Mother, Vol. 2

The People Called Apache

Dog Soldiers, Bear Men, and Buffalo Women

Sundancing at Rosebud and Pine Ridge

Secret Native American Pathways - a Guide to Inner Peace

Exploring the Secret Pathways

ORDERING INFORMATION

THE FOLLOWING PUBLICATIONS RELATED TO FOOLS CROW CAN be found in bookstores and libraries throughout the United States, and some of them are available in Canada, Germany, England, and Australia. They can also be ordered from the following publishers:

Fools Crow
University of Nebraska Press
901 North 17th Street
Lincoln, Nebraska, 68588-0520, USA
telephone: 402-472-3584.

Secret Native American Pathways —
A Guide to Inner Peace
Council Oak Books
1428 South St. Louis Avenue
Tulsa, Oklahoma, 74120, USA
telephone: 1-800-247-8850.

Fools Crow record, tape, and disc,
Etherean Music
4685 Gordon Drive
Boulder, Colorado, 80303, USA
telephone: 1-800-456-5444.

Sundancing at Rosebud and Pine Ridge
The Pathways Foundation
31975 Ortega Highway
Lake Elsinore, California, 92330,
USA, telephones: 714-678-2786,
and 714-678-3996.

Special transcendence, peace and creativity products by Thomas E. Mails that are related to Fools Crow's teaching are also available, and are described in a free brochure that can be obtained by writing to the Pathways Foundation.